▶ **Foucault on the Politics of *Parrhesia***

Other Palgrave Pivot titles

Bernice M. Murphy: *The Highway Horror Film*

Jolene M. Sanders: *Women in Narcotics Anonymous: Overcoming Stigma and Shame*

Patrick Alan Danaher, Andy Davies, Linda De George-Walker, Janice K. Jones, Karl J. Matthews, Warren Midgley, Catherine H. Arden, Margaret Baguley: *Contemporary Capacity-Building in Educational Contexts*

Margaret Baguley, Patrick Alan Danaher, Andy Davies, Linda De George-Walker, Janice K. Jones, Karl J. Matthews, Warren Midgley and Catherine H. Arden: *Educational Learning and Development: Building and Enhancing Capacity*

Marian Lief Palley and Howard A. Palley: *The Politics of Women's Health Care in the United States*

Nikhilesh Dholakia and Romeo V. Turcan: *Toward a Metatheory of Economic Bubbles: Socio-Political and Cultural Perspectives*

Tommi A. Vuorenmaa: *Lit and Dark Liquidity with Lost Time Data: Interlinked Trading Venues around the Global Financial Crisis*

Ian I. Mitroff, Can M. Alpaslan and Ellen S. O'Connor: *Everybody's Business: Reclaiming True Management Skills in Business Higher Education*

Helen Jefferson Lenskyj: *Sexual Diversity and the Sochi 2014 Olympics: No More Rainbows*

Laurence Pope: *The Demilitarization of American Diplomacy: Two Cheers for Striped Pants*

P. Carl Mullan: *The Digital Currency Challenge: Shaping Online Payment Systems through US Financial Regulations*

Ana María Relaño Pastor: *Shame and Pride in Narrative: Mexican Women's Language Experiences at the U.S.–Mexico Border*

Manohar Pawar: *Water and Social Policy*

Jennifer Yamin-Ali: *Data-Driven Decision-Making in Schools: Lessons from Trinidad*

Lionel Gossman: *André Maurois (1885–1967): Fortunes and Misfortunes of a Moderate*

Matthew Watson: *Uneconomic Economics and the Crisis of the Model World*

Michael Gray: *Contemporary Debates in Holocaust Education*

Teresa A. Fisher: *Post-Show Discussions in New Play Development*

Judith Baxter: *Double-Voicing at Work: Power, Gender and Linguistic Expertise*

Majid Yar: *Crime, Deviance and Doping: Fallen Sports Stars, Autobiography and the Management of Stigma*

Grace Ji-Sun Kim and Jenny Daggers: *Reimagining with Christian Doctrines: Responding to Global Gender Injustices*

L. H. Whelchel, Jr.: *Sherman's March and the Emergence of the Independent Black Church Movement: From Atlanta to the Sea to Emancipation*

G. Douglas Atkins: *Swift, Joyce, and the Flight from Home: Quests of Transcendence and the Sin of Separation*

David Beer: *Punk Sociology*

Owen Anderson: *Reason and Faith in the Theology of Charles Hodge: American Common Sense Realism*

DOI: 10.1057/9781137368355.0001

palgrave▸pivot

Foucault on the Politics of *Parrhesia*

Torben Bech Dyrberg

palgrave macmillan

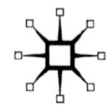

© Torben Bech Dyrberg 2014

All rights reserved. No reproduction, copy or transmission of this publication may be made without written permission.

No portion of this publication may be reproduced, copied or transmitted save with written permission or in accordance with the provisions of the Copyright, Designs and Patents Act 1988, or under the terms of any licence permitting limited copying issued by the Copyright Licensing Agency, Saffron House, 6–10 Kirby Street, London EC1N 8TS.

Any person who does any unauthorized act in relation to this publication may be liable to criminal prosecution and civil claims for damages.

The author has asserted his right to be identified as the author of this work in accordance with the Copyright, Designs and Patents Act 1988.

First published 2014 by
PALGRAVE MACMILLAN

Palgrave Macmillan in the UK is an imprint of Macmillan Publishers Limited, registered in England, company number 785998, of Houndmills, Basingstoke, Hampshire RG21 6XS.

Palgrave Macmillan in the US is a division of St Martin's Press LLC, 175 Fifth Avenue, New York, NY 10010.

Palgrave Macmillan is the global academic imprint of the above companies and has companies and representatives throughout the world.

Palgrave® and Macmillan® are registered trademarks in the United States, the United Kingdom, Europe and other countries.

ISBN: 978–1–13736–836–2 EPUB
ISBN: 978–1–13736–835–5 PDF
ISBN: 978–1–13736–834–8 Hardback

A catalogue record for this book is available from the British Library.

A catalog record for this book is available from the Library of Congress.

www.palgrave.com/pivot

DOI: 10.1057/9781137368355

Contents

List of Illustrations		vi
1	Speaking Truth to Power and Power Speaking Truthfully	1
2	Power: From Productive Submission and Domination to Transformative Capacity	10
3	The Nature of Critique: Political Not Epistemological	31
4	The Politics of Critique: Political Engagement and Government	46
5	The Nature of *Parrhesia*: Political Truth-Telling in Relation to Power, Knowledge and Ethics	66
6	The Politics of *Parrhesia*: The Autonomy of Democratic Politics and the Parrhesiastic Pact	84
7	Leadership and Community: Critique of Obedience and Democratic Paradoxes	102
8	Political Perspectives: Authority and the Duality of Power, Politics and Politicization	119
References		126
Index		137

DOI: 10.1057/9781137368355.0001

List of Illustrations

Figures

2.1 Foucault's categorization of power: relations between freedom/domination (vertical axis) and use/abuse of power (horizontal axis) — 29
4.1 The critical ontology of ourselves vis-à-vis revolutionary vs radical approaches to public political authorities — 60
6.1 Input/output politics in relation to community, regime and authority — 92
7.1 The framing of *parrhesia* — 112

Tables

2.1 Foucault's approach to power, subject and critique in relation to early and late phase — 17
4.1 Contrasting Critical Theory/Ideology Critique and Foucault's political critique — 50
4.2 Two ways of constituting the regulation of public authorities by law — 63

1
Speaking Truth to Power and Power Speaking Truthfully

Abstract: *Foucault's notion of* parrhesia *is tentatively defined and situated in his work where it, among other things, is related to critique.* His interest in parrhesia, *and the reason it is politically relevant, is because it addresses critical issues in democratic theory such as those related to authorities and citizens, what is personal and what is political as well as political ethics and realpolitik. It also touches upon distinctions between input and output politics, which again are related to Foucault's power analytics, and where* parrhesia *is geared to political authorities communicating and implementing their policies.*

Keywords: authority/laypeople; critique; democracy; *parrhesia*; politics; power

Dyrberg, Torben Bech. *Foucault on the Politics of Parrhesia*. Basingstoke: Palgrave Macmillan, 2014.
DOI: 10.1057/9781137368355.0003.

Political *parrhesia* as truthful and trustworthy communication

In this book I will be dealing with Foucault's analyses of the politics of truth-telling as it appear in his lectures (1981–84) and other works, which revolve around the Greek notion of *parrhesia*. If this term could be translated into Latin, it would be *libertas* or *licentia*. *Parrhesia* means speaking truthfully, freely and being up-front in the sense of being open, transparent, engaging and saying everything there is to say about a particular issue in contrast to holding something back, being secretive, covert and manipulative (CT: 218, 326–7; FS: 12; GSO: 381; HS: 372, 404–5). It is a political ethics as opposed to be applied normative theory: it is practical as it is from the outset entwined with government, it is risky and takes timing and courage, it requires knowledge, a good sense of judgement and resolve.

Above all, *parrhesia* is important for Foucault because it operates on the axis of political authorities and citizens vis-à-vis the public realm, it connects personal and institutional aspects of politics and it emphasizes the duty to make sure that words and deeds are not disconnected. In doing so, it stresses trustworthiness and accountability as vital for democracy both personally and institutionally. *Parrhesia* is, moreover, associated with other themes in Foucault's work, notably those related to the enlightenment ethos of critique, the questions of care of self, government and limits to governing as well as liberty as a practice. Finally, it is interesting to see how his focus on *parrhesia* links up with his lifelong academic and political interest in political subjectivation, which orbits around the triangle of power, knowledge and ethics, as well as his libertarian and egalitarian resentment against hierarchical institutional set-ups marked by domination and obedience.

In setting out to discuss *parrhesia* I will be dealing with a set of political issues, which are at once classical themes in political theory and topical and contested issues in today's political culture. *Parrhesia* concerns an individual's freedom to tell the truth, as he or she perceives it after getting acquainted with the facts and due reflection, which is, or rather ought to be, reciprocated by the interlocutor's acceptance of the other's truth-telling. Freedom goes together with courage, because the one who speaks freely and truthfully puts oneself at risk. Thus conceived *parrhesia* links up with public political reasoning, critical engagement, political freedom and personal integrity, which are essential components of a democratic ethos cultivated in a democratic political community. This political aspect of *parrhesia* has captured my attention, and is the major concern for Foucault.

Foucault elaborated in his last series of lectures an approach to political authority and freedom that broke with both mainstream and radical views of the relationship between politics and democracy. In his studies of Greek and Roman antiquity, his implicit message was that Western political discourses have suffered from a negative take on political power, which has resulted in a widespread agreement – irrespective of whether one is right or left, mainstream or radical – that power in general, and political power in particular, is antithetic to truth, fairness, freedom and individuality. This has made democracy appear as a matter of civilizing and depoliticizing the threats of political oppression by converting conflict into consensus and by shielding private individuals from public power. Whilst Foucault on numerous occasions spoke and acted in favour of protecting individuals from repressive power, and saw rights as an indispensable tool in this respect, his primary concern in the lectures was to point out that there could be no democracy unless political authorities, as well as those challenging them, possessed the ability to disconnect politics from their own partial interests and instead tell the population the truth of what has to be done in given situations. This requires that authorities and laypeople are part of a political culture marked by liberty and equality as opposed to domination and hierarchy, which is to say that *parrhesia* and democracy are two sides of the same coin. 'For there to be democracy', says Foucault (GSO: 155), 'there must be *parresia*; for there to be *parresia* there must be democracy. There is a fundamental circularity.'

The argument I develop in this book is that *parrhesia* is vital for Foucault's sustained efforts over the years to expose and criticize the various forms of obedience – be that blatant repression or normalization – which go hand in hand with elite rule, hierarchical structures and states of domination. His interest in *parrhesia* taps into his experiential political inclination to widen and deepen liberty as a practice. The focus is, as it always was for him, on political authorities and their critics. As such *parrhesia* is located right at the centre of Foucault's many histories, because it addresses the key axis of these stories, namely the relationship between authorities and laypeople in all kinds of institutionalized settings such as medical or penal institutions or security apparatuses. Although not formally political, they do partake, according to Foucault, in making up the political infrastructure of society. To put it in more general terms, I will hold that *parrhesia*, as discussed by Foucault, is vital to unlock the nature of the relations between political authorities and the wider political community vis-à-vis regime structures. This is important with regard to assessing the democratic political culture, which involves the resolve of political authorities in doing what has to be done and the political capital of the citizenry to monitor and ultimately control these authorities.

Curiously, no one has to my knowledge pinpointed the twin aspects of political power and critique in Foucault's argument: that to speak truth to power and that power is able to speak truthfully are two sides of the same coin. However, this silence might not be surprising granted the prevailing realist mood of the political science establishment and the defeatist countercultural critical ethos. The self-professed cynicism of both strands of thinking is antithetic to Foucault's discussions of *parrhesia*. Truth-telling in the face of danger, be that of public opinion or repressive authorities, holds a door open for the possibility, unlikely no doubt, that those who wield power actually are able to act in a way that focuses on what the problem at hand requires in contrast to indulging in narrow self-interests while paying lip-service to shared values and sentiments. Hence, *parrhesia* might be the language and practice of both powerful political authorities and their fiercest critics. Contrary to elitist, revolutionary and cynical attitudes, Foucault's approach to political truth-telling implies that truth and power are neither antithetic nor united. And in contrast to mainstream and critical sentiments he is keen to emphasize that *parrhesia* as the serious, clearheaded and critical engagement accentuates that political power cannot be defined exhaustively in negative terms as conflicts of interests, domination, hierarchy and so on.

Foucault's multifaceted discussions of *parrhesia* form an antidote to mainstream as well as to critical approaches. For despite the post-trends' questioning of nearly everything from the late 1970s and up to the 1990s, they left untouched two of the most significant axioms of political science/sociology/theory/philosophy, namely that power is a form of domination, which entails repression one way or the other, and that politics is identified with conflicts over vested interests and/or identities. In both cases we are presented with end-of-politics visions of freedom and emancipation and their corollary, the defeatist 'post' sentiment of being inevitably entangled in cynical power politics where no escape is possible.

Foucault's grasp of power and politics is markedly different. Politics might, of course, involve conflict just as power might involve domination. Most often they do, but they do not have to. Foucault's alternative is twofold. First, he understands politics as orbiting around structures and exercises of the power of authority on the authority/laypeople axis; and he sees power as a transformative capacity both expressing and shaping our ability to act, which is to say that power is a dispositional concept. Second, he deals with politics and power in a way that advances beyond standard scenarios of interest group and identity politics by focusing on the output politics of how it takes effect as opposed to the input politics of, say, representation and deliberation. In addition, from a Foucauldian outlook political power can be innovative and empowering, and can help people to extend their practices of freedom and to govern themselves. This is part of the story of *parrhesia* addressing both political authorities and laypeople.

The politics of truth-telling reveals a surprising turn in Foucault's thinking given his reputation for endorsing a radical view of oppositional politics and a relativistic approach to truth. If there were no other alternatives in political history than the elitist scenario of either dominating others or being dominated, the point of arguing that things could have been done otherwise would be curtailed by an essentialist frame. This would be a vicious circle of domination that would be antithetic to citizens' practicing their political freedom. Just as the quality of democracy relies on political authorities being trustworthy and telling the truth, so the politics of truth depends on laypeople speaking and acting freely, thereby over time building up their political capital. These two levels of truth-telling are far more important than critical theory's insistence that since political power entails conflict and domination, it has to be framed by institutionally defined rules of conduct, just as it has to be legitimate, pluralist, tolerant, respectful of minorities and so on.

Foucault's rejoinder to this kind of argument is to point out that disciplinary subjection with its command/obedience relations is still coercive no matter how democratic state and civil society may be. This means that the idea that liberty flows from protecting personal and civic life from state power by combining a system of individual liberties (rights) with a consensual civic culture (duties) is a depoliticizing illusion, which dodges the essential political relations expressed in the two levels of truth-telling. His argument is, moreover, that disciplinary subjection, with its production of 'docile bodies', is not enough to sustain a politics of truth. The reason is that the latter has to deal with members of a political community who possess some degree of political efficacy and who do not simply do what they are supposed to do either because they do not want to or because they do not know how to do.

To sum up, what Foucault sets out to clarify is that the egalitarian and libertarian ethos of democracy is incompatible with hierarchical structures of obedience, because they thwart practices of liberty and create a culture of conformity, fear in others and lack of trust in oneself. In addition to this ethos of democracy, Foucault also highlights that although *parrhesia* and democracy are two sides of the same coin, they are also at odds with each other, because *parrhesia* differentiates by elevating some above the rest. This raises the issues of ascendance and ethical differentiation, which take the discussion of democracy's liberty/equality a step further by relating it to the necessity of political leadership. Thus Foucault presents us with two types of critique – and *parrhesia* is the archaic form of critique – operating at the authority/citizen axis: criticism of a culture of obedience in the political community and criticism of incompetent and narrow-minded leadership among authorities. Finally, in contrast to both mainstream and radical traditions, which are occupied with, for instance, constitutional set-up, representation, interests group politics, recognition and deliberation, Foucault's discussions of *parrhesia* focus attention on the output side of political processes where decisions are delivered and take effect. Although the discussions of *parrhesia* do testify to certain changes in Foucault's take on agency and action, it does continue his practical focus on how power works – the various technologies that go into forming normalized as well as capable individuals – which is linked up with 'effective history'.

Beyond mainstream and radical approaches

Foucault did not see himself as a political theorist as he no doubt saw this tradition as complicit to the repressive view of power found in the juridico-discursive representation of power, which still had not cut off the head of the king (HS1: 88–9); and he praised Nietzsche as 'the philosopher of power, a philosopher who managed to think of power without having to confine himself within a political theory in order to do so' (PT: 53). In spite of these remarks it might, nonetheless, be tempting to think that he later on began to think of himself as a kind of political theorist by moving into the terrain of political theory and changing it. In any case, what matters is that he breaks with the widespread view found in theories of democracy to think that politics must be domesticated and separated from peoples' life by legal and political means, if they are to enjoy their individual autonomy and social solidarity in relative freedom from political power struggles.

The challenge is to conceptualize the links between the powers of political authorities and the political capital of citizens in the political community in such a way that tensions and paradoxes of democracy, such as those arising between capable leadership and the democratic ethos of equality, are played out politically, and that the political scene is granted autonomy. To put it differently, Foucault's intent is not to insulate politics, and it is not to launch a protective view of democracy. It is to spell out the democratic necessity that public political reasoning and interaction must be, as Rawls would say, 'freestanding'.

Foucault also takes notice of a family resemblance between mainstream and critical political theory in that they both study the relation between politics and democracy as a matter of converting conflict into consensus. As a result, their political analyses are biased towards the input side of political issues, which is expressed in two lines of enquiries. First, the constitutional and normative questions concern how to tame political power to guarantee free and equal access to political decision-making processes. The second deals with interest and identity politics. The former focuses on the distribution of values for a society and the struggles this gives rise to, which is the traditional stuff of political science, and the latter deals with creating identities in relation to more recent issue areas, which are geared to recognition and which are less marked by party politics. The post-trends from the late 1980s emphasizing difference and that everything in context belong to this last category. The point here is not, of course, to downplay the importance to input politics, but to draw attention to the fact that Foucault's contribution to political theory is placed in the output category related to how power as a transformative capacity actually does transform society, for example, when political authorities grasp the moment of opportunity to act, when they respond to risks and crises and when they proactively do what they deem necessary.

Foucault's analyses of political authority and power relations were not conducted independently of his understanding of what it meant to engage in critique. Whilst the critical ethos for his earlier work was associated with the figure of power/resistance, in which power as discipline was seen in terms of productive submission operating in the shadow of sovereignty, his later efforts to analyse the autonomy of politics and the political field gave way for another dimension of critical engagement. This is so because Foucault made it more explicit that he studied political power from the inside according to logics of governing instead of as a trade-off between sovereignty and disciplinary power. This inside-out approach made it possible for him to envisage political power in terms other than the juridical and bellicose models.

My angle to discussing Foucault's *parrhesia*

Although there are books on Foucault dealing with critique, enlightenment, freedom and governing self and others, the book I am presenting here differs in at least three respects. First, it revolves around Foucault's analyses of *parrhesia*, which it sets out to systematize and make sense of in the light of how it contributes to an understanding of the autonomy of the political terrain, which forms the ground for democratic politics. This is a topic that is typically neglected by Foucault scholars. It is also one that opens Foucault's discussions to the works of, amongst others, Arendt and Rawls. I am not pursuing this kind of enquiry here, but there are obvious affinities between them especially with regard to their take on the autonomy of political practice, which would make comparative analyses both relevant and interesting. Second, I set out to study Foucault as a political theorist looking at what he has to say about relations between authorities and laypeople in a democracy, and which role *parrhesia* plays here. This raises the issues of how political authorities and political community are linked, and how personal and institutional aspects of politics are entwined. *Parrhesia* is a way to approach these issues, because it cuts across otherwise entrenched divisions between personal and political, leadership and citizenship, ethics and realpolitik, and so forth. Third, the way in which I deal with issues, such as power/domination, critique/freedom, authority/community and government/*parrhesia*, differ from most of the interpretations I have come across in both mainstream and critical approaches, notably that a defining feature of politics is conflict, that its subject matter is that of vested interests and constructions of identity, and that power can only be thought of in terms of domination in its manifold forms.

In the light of these three points, what I offer in this book is a discussion of a largely neglected topic in Foucault's work: Foucault in the unusual role of political theorist and the portrayal of him in a different light. This should make it a fairly unusual book, which, from an interdisciplinary perspective, addresses both classical issues in political theory and topical ones related to democratic challenges today.

Let me wrap up this introduction with a few words on how I approach Foucault's discussions of *parrhesia* – in fact, Foucault's own words as to how he read Nietzsche (PT: 53–4):

> I prefer to utilise the writers I like. The only valid tribute to thought such as Nietzsche's is precisely to use it, to deform it, to make it groan and protest. And if commentators then say that I am being faithful or unfaithful to Nietzsche, that is of absolutely no interest.

Besides the fact that being faithful or not is irrelevant to scholarly work, the point of bringing this quote is to assert that my primary aim with this book has not been to write a comprehensive introduction to how Foucault dealt with the many aspects of the phenomenon of *parrhesia*. I am, needless to say, concerned with getting his arguments right and grasping what he is getting at, but my overall concern has been to look into how Foucault's discussion of this concept together with a number of others, primarily power and critique, addresses issues of critical importance for today's political orientation. In addition, I have been interested in drawing attention to how far-reaching and radical Foucault's explorations are for common-sense conceptions of politics and power among those who consider themselves critical as opposed to mainstream.

2
Power: From Productive Submission and Domination to Transformative Capacity

Abstract: *The chapter outlines how Foucault's take on power and politics advances beyond traditional parameters in political and democratic theory in which power is typically seen as a type of domination and hence opposed to truth and freedom, just as politics is seen as the prerogative of elites. Focus is centred on how the later Foucault slides away from his earlier emphasis on power as productive submission, and moves towards viewing power as a dispositional concept of being able to act, which can be employed by both repressive and facilitating political technologies. This change of focus links up with his efforts of analysing the autonomy of political practice in general and critical engagement, government and parrhesia in particular.*

Keywords: agonism; autonomy; discipline; domination; politics; power; resistance; transformative capacity

Dyrberg, Torben Bech. *Foucault on the Politics of Parrhesia*. Basingstoke: Palgrave Macmillan, 2014. DOI: 10.1057/9781137368355.0004.

Foucault's approach to power

Foucault had on a number of occasions expressed reservations against coming up with a *theory* of power, because theory, according to him, would entail a prior objectivity of power (SP: 209; see also RM: 148–50). It is not clear why this must be so, and he was, in any case, not consistent in this respect. The notion 'power analytics' would better capture his analytical and historical curiosity as to how we turn out the way we do. What matters is that Foucault set out to analyse power as the ability to act, which is practical through and through and which takes form in relation to forming the self and truth-telling. This is the triangle of power, knowledge and the subject, which delineates the parameters of the experiential field of politics.

It might not look as if Foucault's formalized take on power as the ability to do or effect something has much to offer in terms of analytical purchase. Yet, I will hold that it is significant as a matrix framing analyses of power, which has a number of advantages for understanding among other things the nature of power (Dyrberg 1997: 93–9). This includes whether it is a form of domination, critique seen in relation to limit/transgression, which links up with resistance, and the carving out of a political field of practice, which is related to knowledge and ethics. At this junction I will mention briefly three aspects of Foucault's analyses of power, which are especially relevant: power signals becoming, it is an overarching concept and it delineates context.

Three points are important here. First, the subject *qua* power is becoming of ability via practices. The idea is, says Foucault (TP: 117) in relation to the making of the subject, 'to arrive at an analysis which can account for the constitution of the subject within a historical framework'. Power is essentially involved in this constitution, which is to say that the ability of a subject – be that an individual or an institution – is cultivated and enhanced via technologies and techniques ingrained in institutionally regularized practices. This is the case, for instance, when individuals are caught up in routine processes of disciplinary surveillance the aim of which is efficiency, normalization, accountability, and so forth. These capacities to act are not there beforehand, meaning they are not merely resources one might draw upon, although they do become ingrained in practices as resources over time. It is an unspecified capacity, an ontology of potentials, which is inculcated via training, but which is also presupposed as the target and training ground. It is, in other words, the point of perpetual recurrence that is posed as well as presupposed in practices. In the case of discipline we are dealing with a type of power, which might be characterized as productive submission. Foucault also deals with other types of training and learning, which are involved in political practices, such as the governmentality of bio-politics and security in modern societies and that of bold and risky truth-telling in antiquity, which link up with taking care of oneself when governing others. It also holds for the building of institutional capacities with regard to maximizing output most efficiently and to make people able to do something they were not able to do before.

Second, power as the ability to make a difference is an overarching way of grasping power, which indicates that practices do something to one's ability to comprehend and reflect, interact, decide, perform and evaluate. To put it differently, these abilities take form in practices, and whether they enable and facilitate individuals or institutions to do certain things they might not otherwise would have been able to do or, in contrast, constrain and cripple their capacities and lock them into states of domination where their freedom is seriously curtailed, cannot be inferred from being part of a relation of power. Nor do the mere existence of power relations say anything as to whether we are looking at a situation marked by conflict or consensus, which is, in any case, a typology Foucault is critical of. In both cases we are looking at sub-categories of power, which cannot be entailed by power as a generic category. These are ways of structuring social relations that are contingent upon strategies, contexts and circumstances. Thus conceived, it would be a reductionist mistake to extrapolate specific types of power to *the* form of power and it would, moreover, be to disregard the strictly relational and contingent nature of power relations. This way of grasping the forming of capacities vis-à-vis practices fits into Foucault's various analyses of power from, say, disciplinary normalization to care of the self.

Third, Foucault's relational approach to power as a dispositional concept of being able to do something – or as a transformative capacity[1] – requires a specification of the context in which it is exercised. The structuring of the ability to act, which can be employed by a large variety of political technologies in all sorts of settings and situations, forms and situates practices of agency and hence patterns of identity and signification. The emphasis on context moreover draws attention to an early theme in Foucault's work, namely that of limit and transgression, which he picks up later in relation to archaeological and genealogical dimensions of critique. This theme, which I deal with in Chapter 4, is a matrix for outlining certain practices with their specific rules and codes of conduct, on the one hand, and to see how these rules and codes are subverted, diverted or otherwise undergo changes in negotiations and struggles, on the other. In addition to this discussion of context, Foucault's assertion that power 'is the name that one attributes to a complex strategical situation in a particular society' is relevant for getting at his approach to power immanent in the field it operates and as ubiquitous and relational.[2] His nominalistic point is that it does not attain the status of an object, as it is the overall effect of practices, which situates particular strategies. In addition, the statement is geared to get at agonistic power struggles in which strategies and calculations play an obvious role, as well as the creation of the political field as a semi-autonomous type of practice, which is the foundation for democracy. Finally, it is relevant for discussing critique in general and truth-telling (*parrhesia*) in particular.

Having mentioned these three aspects of Foucault's approach to power, let me briefly outline what I intend to do in this chapter. I will start by taking a summary look at some of the typical approaches and dichotomies to be found in power theories, which will set the stage for assessing what Foucault has on offer by questioning what we look for when studying power and how we approach power. The idea is to outline how Foucault's take on power and politics advances beyond traditional parameters in democratic theory in which power is typically seen as a type of domination opposed to truth and freedom, just as politics is seen as the prerogative of elites, which make up the political stratum and their contenders, that is, people who are knowledgeable and capable. Foucault's arguments concerning critical engagement, government and *parrhesia* are important antidotes to this line of enquiry as they are linked to his efforts of analysing the autonomy of political practice and to the political logics of governing, organized around the axis of authorities and laypeople and viewed through the lenses of the power/ knowledge/subject triangle instead of interests. He distances himself not only from mainstream political science/sociology/philosophy but also from critical approaches, because they see conflicts of interests as the essence of politics. In contrast, the focus and locus of Foucault's power analytics is different. He works with various types of power operating at the macro level, such as sovereign power and later bio-politics and security; he differentiates between using and abusing power as well as between strategical games of liberties and states of domination; and he relates power and government to political reasoning and its moral implications. In addition, he does not locate political power in the input category of elite groups struggling to get the upper hand when it comes to 'who gets what, when, and how' (the title of Lasswell's book from 1936), which is the interest group politics we find in pluralist and elitist approaches.

In light of the fact that both mainstream and critical approaches assume that power entails domination, one way or the other, and that politics is unthinkable without conflicts of interests and/or identity, it will be relevant to take a look at how Foucault deals with the issue of domination. Is it an inescapable feature of power relations that they will always lead to the submission of the many, or is it possible to play the game of power in such a way as to minimize the effects of domination/submission? Questions on these lines were not answered by Foucault's doubts about and bracketing of the repressive hypothesis (HS1: 10–12, part two), which was a critique of the legal modelling of power centred around denial and prohibition where a fully constituted subject was encroached upon by power from the outside, as it were. In disciplinary technologies of power, the subject came into being as productive and submissive. This formed the political drive of his analyses of disciplinary society, which was portrayed as repressive albeit productive.

So the question is whether, or the extent to which, domination is essentially involved in power relations. I do not think Foucault was clear on this point, although it is possible to trace a development in his arguments from the early 1970s to 1984. This is illustrated in the three 'power and domination' sections below. The point is that we move from (1) an approach to power in which power is seen in terms of domination, which in Foucault's work takes the form of the productive submission by means of disciplinary power and where history is seen as a series of changing forms of domination to (2) one in which domination is but one pole in power relations, which can be played down. This implies a more open-ended scenario of power relations and struggles just as it gives way for political as well as ethical dimensions, which are vital for dealing with the politics of *parrhesia*. Moreover, whereas the subject in the first scenario is largely in the receiving end of power relations, it is given a creative role in the latter. This change of perspective is, as I argue throughout this book, closely linked to Foucault's focus on power as government, which he studies in relation to political authorities and the self vis-à-vis others.

The politics of theorizing power

It goes for power theories in general and for Foucault in particular that the academic interest in conceptualizing power is often entwined with taking a political stance and being actively involved in politics. In his comments to the community power debates, starting in the 1950s in the USA, Lukes (2005: 1; see also Morriss 1987: 41–2; 2006: 128–30) mentions that 'how to think about power theoretically and how to study it empirically' links up with the political question of 'how to characterize American politics'. The key issue in these debates was whether politics was pluralist or dominated by ruling elites. Moreover, in discussing the three faces of power – from Dahl et al. via Bachrach and Baratz and further to Lukes himself – he associated them with a liberal, reformist and radical approach, respectively (Lukes 2005: 37–8). The point is not to take issue with this heuristic, but rather crude, way of linking intellectual and political work, but to suggest that Foucault's power analytics as it took form in the mid-1970s was no exception to forging this kind of connection between political radicalism and scholarly work. His work on early modern society in *Discipline and Punish* from 1975 arose in a highly politicized environment in which leftist activists were looking for novel ways to understand the workings of power in daily life in late-modern societies. For several strands of the new left – including Foucault and his Maoist associates – it made not much sense to try to derive structures of domination/obedience from the class-struggle as the Marxist would have it, although Marxism, however conceived, was the language of radicals (Wolin 2010: 296). Foucault's contribution had political ramifications for a whole generation of critically minded students and academics whose oppositional identity was nourished by Foucault's way of conceptualizing the ubiquity of power relations as productive submission, his allegedly cynical and relativistic linking of power and knowledge and his anarchic appraisal of resistance carried out by subjugated and marginalized individuals and groups. Dahl's comments on the sentiments of those endorsing 'the ruling elite model' – leftists criticizing the status quo – fit in appropriately here. Radical elite theory as well as Foucault's approach to power as productive submission in the early 1970s appealed to 'individuals with a strong strain of frustrated idealism' as they both had 'just the right touch of hard-boiled cynicism' (Dahl 1968: 25).

The aura of radicalism surrounding his work on power as discipline is in no way matched by his later works on power, knowledge and ethics in Greek and Roman antiquity. Several reasons might account for this change:

- That leftist radicalization had faded out by the early/mid-1980s;
- That the subject matter was conceived as too remote for present-day concerns;
- That leftist academics saw his new investigations on the care of the self and *parrhesia* as entangled in individual ethics and aesthetics;
- That the view of power emerging in his later works was not coined in terms of power/resistance so dear to oppositional identification and
- That the view of politics, likewise, had changed from administering disciplinary society to becoming a field practicing equality and freedom.

Especially the last two points indicated that Foucault increasingly came to look at political power as a transformative capacity rather than as some form of domination, which could easily entice criticism and thus confirm a critical stance. The overall reception of these changes in Foucault's work as well as in the *Zeitgeist* of postmodern fatigue from the late 1980s onwards are inseparable from an increasing sense of political disorientation.

In my opinion, Foucault pursues a more radical and profound investigation of both power and politics, which extends his enduring curiosity in forms of power that are irreducible to its juridico-discursive representation, whilst at the same time reconsidering the nature of power and politics. In doing so he questions not only mainstream assumptions in political science, but also self-styled radicals who do in actual fact operate with the same mind set: that power is repressive and that politics – or in radical conservative and leftist parlance: 'the political' – entails conflict, antagonism, enmity and the like. In addition, Foucault's analyses of power, knowledge and ethics in antiquity ought to have consequences for the ways in which we view political authority and democratic politics today. This is to suggest that Foucault did not engage in these discussions merely as a learned scholar who wanted to throw light on, among other things, *parrhesia* and the care of the self.

TABLE 2.1 *Foucault's approach to power, subject and critique in relation to early and late phase*

	Power	Subject	Critique
Early phase	Productive submission: surveillance and discipline entail normalization	Passive: 'docile body' Active: obstruction, insubordination, the outsider	Outside-in: unmasking the system, power vs resistance
Late phase	Creative capacity: from coercive to also being facilitating	Active: forming itself vis-à-vis knowledge, power and ethics, part of the authority/ laypeople axis	Inside-out: engagement, reflexive, negotiation and avoidance

He was also a kind of political activist who gave the power/knowledge/ethics triangle a new twist in his defence for democratic political reasoning in the 'the open society'. This is Foucault's challenge, which is both intellectual and political, and radicals ought to pick it up!

Foucault, the scholar and political activist, was of a much different bent back in the early 1970s, which can be illustrated by taking a look at how his arguments concerning power and domination developed. Although there are no clear-cut stages, there are differences in the ways he deals with power, the subject and critique due to changing orientations and emphases from the early 1970s to the early 1980s. This is illustrated tentatively in Table 2.1, which contrasts early and late phases, but one should keep in mind that it might be more fruitful to speak of orientation and foci instead of stages.

Power and domination: the straightjacket

In the early/mid-1970s, Foucault's political involvement as a revolutionary leftist political intellectual was triggered by his resentment against what he and significant segments of the 1968 generation saw as a technocratic and authoritarian system, which could not be adequately understood and fought against by using the economistic Marxist categories of social classes and the demise of capitalism. Instead, with *Discipline and Punish* he saw late-modern society as an extrapolation of the prison, which focused on the ordinary and practical effects of power. He launched a critique of the system of authoritarian political power that was fortified by the productive submission of the body, which in turn was generated by disciplinary technologies.[3] Power as discipline was both productive and repressive as its rationale was to form the individual as efficient and reliable. As this was, ultimately, impossible, there would always be points of insubordination and obstruction, which operated as vehicles for new exercises of power. Power and resistance were thus two sides of the same coin, meaning that resistance was defined as power encountering or clashing with another power in consequence of which it was impossible to differentiate them qualitatively (Brökling et al. 2011: 19; Hook 2007: 84–5).

Repression and domination were the motivation to criticize and resist, which were made possible by the impossibility of the system to fully normalize people, that is, to control everything and leave no room for freedom. Although the omnipresence of power did not mean that systemic power was omnipotent, it was, nonetheless, far from obvious if it mattered to put up resistance as it would seem near impossible to break out of the disciplinary straightjacket. Although Foucault tried to escape the either/or of 'the promise of "liberation"' and 'you are always-already trapped' (HS1: 83), disciplinary subjection seemed to be an historical a priori, which meant that resistance eventually could not but confirm this type of power. This would indicate that power as domination, which 'controls everything and leaves no room for freedom' (ESF: 293), was after all inescapable, which was a much debated issue amongst numerous critical authors mainly of a Marxist bent for whom Foucault's approach stunned attempts to resist power, which in turn would render Emancipation futile.[4] These critics might well have a point, and Foucault's sketchy attempts to flesh out what resistance actually meant and what it looked like did not appear convincing. This would go for his brief mentioning of, for instance that '[t]he rallying point for the counterattack against the deployment of sexuality ought not to be sex-desire, but bodies and pleasures' and that 'plebs' as 'an inverse energy, a discharge' is 'the permanent, ever silent target for apparatuses of power'.[5] However, it should be remembered that what Foucault no doubt had in mind was that it would be 'self-defeating to attempt to oppose discipline and normalization by recourse to the language of rights and sovereignty' (Simons 1995: 54; see also Doxiadis 1997: 534), because this language was the other side of the disciplinary coin. Disciplinary technologies escaped, in other words, the radar of rights, or, more to the point, rights relied on individuals being made accountable by these technologies.

Foucault was not burdened by a Marxist eschatological vision of the withering away of political power. In going back to 'Nietzsche, Genealogy, History' from 1971, he expressed himself in line with one of the most persistent postulates of classical continental European elitism when he spoke of 'the endlessly repeated play of domination' where class domination among other things 'generates the idea of liberty'.[6] This idea was a way of hiding the real nature of class rule behind the facade of rights and obligations, just as progress was a hoax hiding the cyclical nature of time in which 'humanity installs each of its violences in a system of rules and thus proceeds from domination to domination' (NGH: 151). Following this Nietzschean lead, domination and violent hierarchies were inescapable, only their form and content would undergo changes in different societies at different times: powerful regimes would crumple and others take over, one way of repressing people would be replaced by others, and so on, *ad infinitum*. Behind the facade of grandiose values and eschatological ideologies, this was at the end of the day nothing but the never-ending game of getting power over others, which meant that it was only possible to conceive of power as domination, repression, a means to wage war, and so forth (Neocleous 1996: 83–6). It was this timeless and hence transcendental scheme that framed power in general and political power in particular. In addition, Foucault claimed that every form of social unity – including that of the subject – could only be seen in terms of struggle and submission, which was the motor of history and hence the functional principle of society. In arguing on those lines, Foucault implicitly asserted that difference entails hierarchy at least in a political context and that power and politics were inextricably linked up with domination, war and conflict. The problem with statements such as these is that although Foucault is adamant to insist that power is relational, it is, nonetheless, framed a priori by domination. He revised this position later on as it was incompatible with his genealogical stress on contingency. He did so, partly by focusing on the context of power relations in which he differentiated between strategical games of liberty and states of domination, and partly by looking at power apart from its particular manifestations, in which he occasionally allowed for power relations not being repressive.

The issue of resistance in Foucault's work is a tricky one, and it illustrates the entwined nature of his scholarly and political motivation: *analytically*, resistance is the other side of power, which keeps it going; *politically* it is the opposite of obedience and submission, which are his main targets of criticism. One might say that Foucault was confronted with two sets of criticism. First, he was criticized for *de facto* rendering resistance to power impossible, partly, due to the fact that he never systematically analysed forms of resistance to power, but paid almost exclusive attention to understanding institutionalized forms of power relations such as the productive submission of disciplinary technologies, and partly because his conception of power as constitutive and omnipresent made it irrelevant to look for pockets of resistance, a revolutionary identity, that were not, as yet, marked by power. To ward off this kind of critique – that resistance was impossible or did not matter – he would insist not only on resistance being an irreducible part of power relations, which would somehow modify those relationships, but also that it attained priority in power relations. The issue of domination and resistance is expressed in an interview from 1982. Foucault states, 'You have to use power relations to refer to the situation where you're not doing what you want. So resistance comes first, and resistance remains superior to the forces of the process.' Hence '*resistance* is the main word, *the key word*, in this dynamic' (SPI: 167). This statement boils down to the assertion that power is domination (the thwarting of will) and that resistance conditions power.

It is noteworthy that Foucault uses power to designate a situation where one does something one does not want to do. This is surprising given the fact that he had on earlier occasions been critical of this way of looking at power in terms of prohibition and will. For example, in an interview from 1978 he criticized approaches to power as 'what prohibits, what prevents people doing something. It seemed to me that power was something much more complex than that' (OP: 102). Surprising or not, the point is that this take on power gets resistance going and even institutes it as the primal category as it designates an experience of discomfort that entices a reaction, and it is this, which defines a relation as a power relation. It might then be possible to argue that Foucault's way of dealing with resistance as 'the key word' suggests that it is a name for the dynamic nature of power relations, that their modus of existence is unfixity and changeability. This leaves resistance unspecified, as the underside of power and, as he would say later in relation to critique, as countermoves to being governed, 'the art of not being governed like that and at that cost' (WC: 45).

Second, given that it is impossible to imagine power relations that do not involve resistance, one would have to see power as a type of practice that encroaches upon or controls people in such a way that they react against it, which in turn implies that they have a certain degree of freedom to be able to do that in the first place. But what if they do not react? Is it because it is not a power relation anyway? Is it because they do something they do not want to do, they just do not know it? Or is it because they are so repressed that they do not dare put up resistance? These questions are similar to the ones Bachrach and Baratz asked Dahl in the early/mid-1960s when they questioned that the absence of grievances implied consensus. One could not, they argued, rule out by definitional fiat that consensus had been manufactured in the interest of ruling elite groups. Be that as it may, one of the problems with this line of argument is that the existence of power is made dependent upon the reactions it entices and that it is not clear what the reaction implies, how to detect it and hence what it means to resist. Another problem is that it cannot avoid being a reductionist account of power: a contingent aspect of power is turned into an essential one, as it only gets at one aspect of power, however important, namely that of struggle triggered by being subordinated. Foucault did change that, although he never really let go of the view that power is caught up with domination. One way of posing the question of resistance is whether it defines a power relationship or is likely to go hand in hand with power relations. He seems to go for the former, yet he increasingly paid attention to practices of creative individuals, which, so it would seem, went hand in hand with analysing power in ways that did not gravitate around tactics and techniques of domination/subjugation.

Power and domination: loosening up

Power is, says Weber (1978: 53, see also 926), 'the probability that one actor within a social relationship will be in a position to carry out his own will despite resistance, regardless of the basis on which this probability rests'. Power is 'sociologically amorphous', because it is omnipresent and because 'domination in the quite general sense of power, i.e., of the possibility of imposing one's own will upon the behavior of other persons, can emerge in the most diverse forms' (Weber 1978: 942, see also 53). To define power along these lines, Weber assumes that power is power only if it meets resistance *and* suppresses it, which is to say that resistance is necessary for power, but that it also has to play a subordinate role – it is as Derrida would say a 'dangerous supplement' (1976: part II, ch. 2). Power as domination entails clashes between wills/interests, and these conflicts can only be solved through subjection that institutes a hierarchy of domination. *Herrschaft* is seen as domination by virtue of authority, which concerns 'the probability that a *command* will be obeyed' (Weber 1978: 53, 943) and can only be thought of as a particular way of structuring power that is able to bend resistance. This is the political imperative implied in the conflict/consensus approach, which means that the role and hope of democracy is to render political domination legitimate.

In turning to Foucault's take on power and domination, one can start with one of his latest interviews in which he states (ESF: 293): 'The idea that power is a system of domination that controls everything and leaves no room for freedom cannot be attributed to me.' As he himself mentions, everything depends upon how these terms are understood. When seen in relation to Weber's view of domination as a defining trait of power, Foucault's point makes good sense even when we go back to the 1970s where he saw power in terms of the struggle/war/repression scheme. 'We have', he says in his critique of the model of *Leviathan*, 'to analyze it [power] by beginning with the techniques and tactics of domination' and orient the analysis of power to 'forms of subjugation', which are connected 'with apparatuses of knowledge' (SMD: 34; see also TL: 102). Although power is not, strictly speaking, equated with domination, it is the starting point for analyses of power relations and the motivation to put up resistance. The latter is possible because power as domination does not control everything; that is, it does not make up a homogenous bloc. The difference compared to earlier statements is that Foucault does not refer tacitly to domination as a transcendental matrix, which is his way out of the accusation that he had made resistance and freedom impossible.

In relation to Weber's explicit definition of power as a category of domination, Foucault would emphasize three things. First, his main focus had never been to look at decision-makers imposing their will or interest upon others, as he was keener to analyse how will and interest were formed in the first place. That is to say, he was not concerned with 'who exercises power?' but in 'how does it happen?' and 'how it came to be accepted by everybody' (OP: 103–4). It is these 'how' questions that led him to focus on disciplinary normalization as the political anatomy of detail and his later concern with bio-politics and security. Second, he did not assume, contrary to Weber, 'that power is only real or effective where it cannot be resisted, as if the mere fact that an action *elicits* another's resistance were not already proof of the power relation between them' (Allen 1998: 177). The point was to look at the network of power relations, in which individuals were vehicles, as opposed to the isolated net result of exercising power. In addition, he saw, as already mentioned, resistance as the dynamic element in power relations, as that which accounted for change. Finally, in spite of his flirtation with the maxims of elite theory in which domination was the horizon of intelligibility he did underline that power relations were 'strictly relational' as they depended 'on a multiplicity of points of resistance' (HS1: 95). That is why he could not accept to view 'power as a phenomenon of mass and homogeneous domination' (SMD: 29), because even '[m]ajor dominations are the hegemonic effects that are sustained by all these confrontations' (HS1: 94).

For Foucault, the flip side of binding political power to the legal set-up of sovereignty was disciplinary normalization and this meant that he did not take issue with conceptualizing power in terms of domination. His main concern was, instead, to break out of 'the spell of monarchy' symbolizing political thought. The alternative was to 'cut off the head of the king' by moving from right, law and punishment to technique, normalization and control (HS1: 89; TP: 121) thus supplementing the legal model of contract/oppression with the bellicose schema of war/repression (SMD: 15–17; TL: 92). This served the critical purpose of unmasking how power operated beneath the surface where it was not caught up in the edifice of juridical thought and legal constraints, but could operate more freely. Here it was possible to detect what he termed 'the local cynicism of power' (HS1: 95). The critical encounter was worked out within 'a pseudo-military vocabulary', which Foucault had adopted experimentally and somewhat hesitantly (PP: 16). Although he later on questioned and partly abandoned the bellicose approach to power, and hence that domination was intrinsic to power, it did serve another and wider purpose than just critique, if by that we refer to exposing domination dressed up as liberty and equality, namely that of working out the contours of how political authority works. To do that would require that '[w]e must construct an analytics of power that no longer takes law as a model and a code' (HS1: 90)[7] and, more generally, to base political theory on political grounds as opposed to, say, a trade-off between a juridical set-up and social norms (Simons 1995: 52–4). However, he never abandoned the bellicose take on power in a clear-cut manner although he did develop an argument of political power as an autonomous and transformative capacity. This is the power of governing self and others, which went along with another view of critique compared to the one he adopted in the early 1970s.

Foucault was 'eventually forced to reconsider' the struggle/repression scheme (SMD: 17). Even in the mid-1970s where he outlined 'the strategical model' of power to counter 'the legal model', the omnipresence of power did not entail an omnipotent system of domination, one that thoroughly curtailed individual freedom, though this was a disputed issue among his commentators. Foucault did not argue against power being grasped as repression and domination as these terms, quite to the contrary, supplemented the contract/oppression dichotomy that framed the juridical scheme. The critical task, according to Foucault, was to expose 'that the essential function of the discourse and technique of right has been to efface the domination intrinsic to power' and that 'it is therefore designed to eliminate the fact of domination and its consequences' (TL: 95; see also SMD: 26). This task of unmasking official images of power with their representation of individuals as free and equal had an affinity with the Critique of Ideology developed within the Critical Theory tradition. Both aimed at showing that the real mechanisms of power had been covered up as they fitted uneasily with political and academic discourses of rights and liberties, whereas they, in fact, licensed the repression of people.

Power and domination: agonistic encounters

In his commentary to his 1982 course work, Gros mentions, 'for a long time Foucault conceived of the subject as only the passive product of techniques of domination' (Gros 2005: 525; see also Farrell 1989: 39). Foucault himself takes it even further by stating that 'individuality is today completely controlled by power' and that 'our individuality ... is the effect and instrument of power' (Foucault quoted in Paras 2006: 78). In his later works, by contrast, the individual is no longer merely being acted on, that is, formed by the disciplinary mechanisms of productive submission in hierarchically organized institutions. Instead, it forms itself by techniques of the self in the political intersection of power, knowledge and ethics. This change in the way he approached power was part of what might with some reservation be called Foucault's political turn, which is also a change of perspective from looking at the receiving end of power relations to focusing instead on those exercising it over themselves and others. What goes on here could be seen as an implicit distancing from his earlier position in which he gave 'very little room to what you might call the creativity of individuals, to their capacity for creation' as he put it in his debate with Chomsky in 1971 (HN: 15; see also Paras 2006: 78).

With Foucault's development of the political macro approach of biopolitics and security, which was not caught up in the axis of sovereignty and discipline, power is no longer seen exclusively in the bellicose terms of struggle, repression and domination. The power/knowledge that goes into the authorities conducting the behaviour of others by getting them to do something they would not or, perhaps, could not otherwise have done *might* go hand in hand with the exercise of repressive power, just as it *might* result in an intolerable state of domination. But whether this will actually be the outcome is an open question and it is, in any case, a contingent as opposed to an inevitable result of exercising power. The point is not just that power as 'the name one attributes to a complex strategical situation' indicates that power relations are to a greater or lesser extent unstable and reversible, and that this gives way for escape, insubordination and confrontation (SP: 220–1; SKP: 245). It is rather that Foucault later on broadened his perspective on power in general and political power in particular. This is clear in his discussions of government, which 'take into account the interaction between ... techniques of domination and techniques of the self'. This, he saw as 'a kind of autocritique' as he had previously insisted 'too much on the techniques of domination' (ST: 153–4; see also Paras 2006: 94).

Two entwined aspects of power relations are interesting: their context and their nature. With regard to the context he maintained in line with the strategical model of power that it involves a repressive dimension, but he began distinguishing between degrees of freedom ranging from what he called 'strategical games of liberties', where it is possible to put up resistance by evading being governed in this or that way, to 'states of domination', where individuals are locked into hierarchical structures and patterns of repression and left with very few options of manoeuvrability. Seen in this light, power and domination connote a difference between movement and activity, on the one hand, and stasis and passivity, on the other.[8] Concerning the nature of power, he took the more radical step of beginning to see power as a creative capacity, which is an overarching category compared to the different modalities and functions of power – for example, discipline at the micro level and bio-politics at the macro level – that can be either repressive or facilitating. There is an affinity between this aspect and discussions of 'power over' and 'power to', which does not run parallel to conflict and consensus, but indicates that power is the ability to do something.[9] I will come back to this creative aspect of power in the subsequent chapters on critique and *parrhesia*. At this point I will concentrate on the contextual aspect of power as 'a complex strategical situation' by looking at what the continuum of liberty and domination means for Foucault's approach to power.

The reason Foucault mentioned that power as 'a system of domination that controls everything and leaves no room for freedom' could not be attributed to him was to emphasize the strictly relational character of power relations in which power and resistance presupposed each other. 'It would not be possible for power relations to exist', says Foucault (SP: 225), 'without points of insubordination which, by definition, are means of escape.' If power were a system of domination it would be a contradiction of terms because a state of domination would be one in which agents manage 'to block a field of relations of power, to render them impassive and invariable and to prevent all reversibility of movement'. The result would be that 'power relations are fixed in such a way that they are perpetually asymmetrical and allow an extremely limited margin of freedom'.[10] Foucault's antidote to blockage and fixity, that is, to power as 'a massive and primal condition of domination, a binary structure with "dominators" on one side and "dominated" on the other' (PST: 142), is to call attention to resistance as the dynamic element in power relations and to evoke Nietzsche's notion of agonism. The idea is to stress the 'complicated interplay' between power and freedom (SP: 221; see also SPI: 167), which characterizes the adversarial strife that lies at the heart of the strategical model.

What he referred to as a complex strategical situation or a field of interactions is prior to 'power as mastery, as a fundamental given, a unique principle, explanation or irreducible law'. The point is, he goes on, that exercising power 'is associated with a domain of possibility and consequently of reversibility, of possible reversal' (WC: 66). This emphasis on possibility indicates that power cannot after all be boxed into the category of repression, productive submission, and the like, as it can have other effects as well. In addition, it facilitates to pick up a neglected issue in contemporary political thought, namely that of the ethical subject (ESF: 294). The challenge in relation to the topic of ethics, which increasingly occupied Foucault, was to let go of the political subject as the subject of law and fabricated by disciplinary normalization and, instead, elaborate on the ethical subject from a political point of view, which is practical and experimental. This idea went together with that of developing a critical sense in which personal autonomy and integrity form the basis for critique of and resistance against abuses of power and states of domination. Freedom is the other side of power when the latter is seen in non-deterministic terms of possibility and becoming. Freedom is on top of that 'the ontological condition of ethics. But ethics is the deliberate form assumed by liberty' in which power relationships 'must be controlled by practices of freedom'.[11] For this to happen one has to shake up power relations, as it were, so as to prevent them from congealing into states of domination, where the constraints imposed on freedom would be hard to modify. This is a call for an ongoing resistance to domination, which does not, contrary to Habermas, Fraser and others, 'presuppose the normative ideal of a true discourse, in which difference and conflict will be overcome' and result in a 'consensual voice' (Falzon 1998: 88). As I will discuss in relation to critique and *parrhesia* in the next chapters, the political norm is rather that of creating oneself, that is, one's abilities to take care of oneself and, by extension, others by developing one's personal and political integrity. This takes curiosity and an experimental attitude, which advance an understanding of one's historical embeddedness and how to transgress the limitations one encounters.

To distinguish power and domination in terms of degrees of freedom does not alter the fact that Foucault still speaks of power as domination. This is, for instance, clear when he argues that a 'relationship of confrontation reaches its term, its final moment ... when stable mechanisms replace the free play of antagonistic reactions', and then goes on to describe power relations as somebody setting out 'to control the conduct of others' through these 'stable mechanisms' (SP: 225; ESF: 299, see also 292). Moreover, given his way of contrasting active and passive, alias resistance and obedience, he claims, as I have already mentioned, that '[y]ou have to use power relations to refer to the situation where you're not doing what you want' (SPI: 167). This implies to get them to do certain things, which at the same time, limits their freedom. In a statement that resembles Weber when he speaks of 'domination in the quite general sense of power ...', Foucault holds that '[d]omination is in fact a general structure of power' (SP: 226). In pursuing this line of reasoning, Foucault comes close to ways of conceiving power within mainstream political science/sociology, as when he implicitly holds that power and freedom are proportional for those exercising power and inversely proportional for those who are exercised power over.[12] Moreover, to set power and domination apart by degrees of freedom and to see the conduct of subjects as controlled via stable mechanisms, which suspend freedom, would suggest a rather crude affinity between freedom and instability. However, there is something more to these mechanisms, which provides another angle to Foucault's discussion of domination, which seem to be more in line with his critical ethos where political ethics plays a key role.

His liberty/domination continuum ranges from open and reciprocal relations of power to stable and asymmetrical states of domination. As a mediating factor we find governmental rules, rationales and technologies, and it is these governmental technologies of the self that is interesting, because it is here Foucault sets out to distinguish between acceptable and unacceptable forms of power, just as it is here he discusses critique as a way of evading, countering and negotiating attempts to be governed in this or that way. Foucault's distinction between using and abusing power is important for both of these concerns. Whilst the use/abuse of power signals openness and reciprocity vs closure and hierarchy, respectively, it might not necessarily be the case that control and hence the restriction of freedom amounts to abusing power. For this to be the case it would, according to Foucault, have to imply that 'one exceeds the legitimate exercise of one's power and imposes one's fantasies, appetites, and desires on others' as in the cases, for example, 'where a kid is subjected to the arbitrary and unnecessary authority of a teacher, or a student put under the thumb of a professor who abuses his authority' (ESF: 288, 299; see also HS: 375).

Abuses of power lead to states of domination. This is problematic for at least two reasons. First, the freedom of others is constrained to the point that their means to change the system are for all practical purposes eliminated, whereby 'a system of constraint becomes truly intolerable'.[13] This form of constraint might be established by scientific and moral codes, which become ingrained in a system of social stratification and a hierarchical political system. Second, because the criteria for governing others are idiosyncratic, as they cannot be generalized and made public, those in power cannot be held accountable for their conduct. Both of these aspects are important for the subsequent discussions of *parrhesia* and public political reasoning, and they, moreover, suggest that 'Foucault's politics lean toward a radical, agonistic democracy in which liberal freedoms are valued as the necessary conditions for the practice of strategic games of liberty' (Simons 1995: 22).

```
            Strategical game of liberties
```

```
                    ↑
   arbitrary    |   empower
   unpredictable|   facilitate
                |   autonomy
  ──────────────┼──────────────
   tyranny      |   top-down
   dictatorship |   governance
                    ↓
```

Abusing power ← → Using power

States of domination

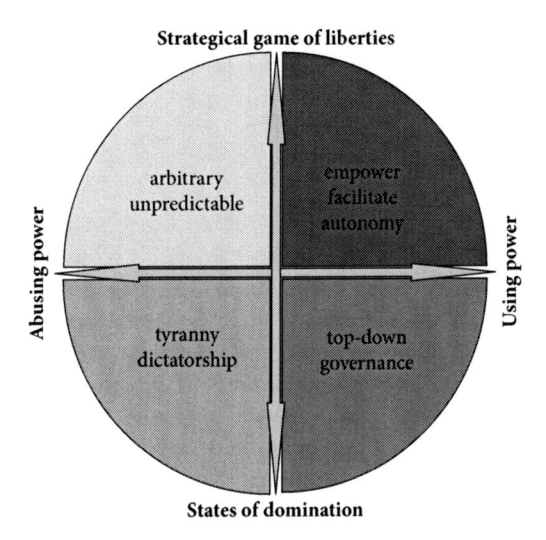

FIGURE 2.1 *Foucault's categorization of power: relations between freedom/ domination (vertical axis) and use/abuse of power (horizontal axis)*

Notes

1   Morriss 1987: 13, 17, 19. Giddens (1979: 92, see also 88–94) is onto the same thing although he holds that power does entail domination: 'power is a relational concept, but only operates as such through t he utilization of transformative capacity as generated by structures of domination'.

2   HS1: 93. See also his elaboration of 'the strategical model' in part IV, ch. 2. A similar statement can be found in DP: 215.

3   Foucault's intellectual and political interest for the prison dates back to 1971 where he played a leading role in forming 'Groupe d'Information sur les Prisons' (GIP). As an object of study, the prison combined his key interest, 'for it would involve not just archives, but also political actions that would lead to his direct engagement with social movements that were to shake up the penal system' (Eribon 1991: 217). Deleuze (1986: 32) shortly alludes to Foucault's timely invention of his new approach to power in his review of *Discipline and Punish*: 'Et quand Foucault revient en 1975 à une publication théorique, il nous semble le premier à inventer cette nouvelle conception du pouvoir, que l'on cherchait sans savoir la trouver ni l'énoncer.' He moreover lists five assumptions about the novelty of Foucault's approach to power (32–8). See also Miller 1994: 222–3; Wolin 2010: 289–90, 296.

4 See, for example, Dews 1986: 97–100; Fine 1979: 91–4; 1984: 189–202; Jameson 1998: 105–8; Jessop 1987: 77, 79, 81–2; 2011: 64; Keat 1986; Neocleous 1996: 79–83; Philp 1983: 43–8; Poulantzas 1978: 77–80, 146–53; Wickham 1986: 156–7, 163–8.
5 HS1: 157; PST: 137–8. For a discussion of 'the plebeian aspect', see also Ransom 1997: 117–33.
6 NGH: 150. Note also his comments in DP: 222 that '[t]he "Enlightenment", which discovered the liberties, also invented the disciplines'. See also SMD: 26–7.
7 There is a parallel between this approach to power and his later distinction between morals and ethics: just as his analytics of power aims to free itself from the legal code and grasp how power relations actually work, so his concern for ethics is a way to create a critical distance to the moral code, which prescribes what is legitimate and what is not in order to get at how people actually live their lives in relation to moral codes.
8 SP: 226; ESF: 283, 292, 299. Laclau and Mouffe (1985: 105) were on to the same thing when they spoke of 'elements' and 'moments' in discourses, which were two ends of a continuum ranging from unfixity to fixity of signification. This couplet has an affinity to Laclau's later distinction inspired by Husserl (Laclau 1990: 33–6) of 'reactivation', which signals dislocation, and 'sedimentation', which is business as usual. Two differences between them should be mentioned. First, Laclau and Mouffe make a distinction between domination and oppression, but it is not of kind but of reception: the latter is the experience of the former as intolerable. Foucault, by contrast, does not differ between them and holds that the very fact of ending up in a state of domination is oppressive irrespective of how people perceive or react to such a state. Second, whereas Laclau equates sedimentation with the social, which is not, by definition, political, Foucault sees the social as political, since it is constituted by the technologies and techniques of governmentality. This is among other things a difference between defining 'the political' in terms of antagonism and authority, respectively.
9 Power is, as I have already mentioned, a 'dispositional concept' (Morris 1987: 19; 2006). See also Patton (1989) for his distinction between the two locutions of power: 'to' and 'over'.
10 ESF: 283, 292, see also 299. In one of his last interviews, Foucault (IA: 399) mentions, 'I am flabbergasted that people are able to see in my historical studies the affirmation of a determinism from which one cannot escape.'
11 ESF: 283–4. For a discussion of this phrase see Oksala 2005: 188–92.
12 Foucault does not phrase it in those terms, but his approach to power is surprisingly similar as we are dealing with a will that is curbed by power and puts up resistance. SP: 221; Clifford 2001: 138–9.
13 SCA: 294. This might well be the case, yet people's perceptions of what constitute constraints differ, so it is not clear where the threshold of the 'truly intolerable' begins.

3
The Nature of Critique: Political Not Epistemological

Abstract: *In contrast to epistemology-based types of critique, such as Ideology Critique, which aim to peel off layers of manipulation to get at the real thing, critique for Foucault is political and is played out at the axis of authorities and laypeople. Critique is negotiated and concerns where to draw the line between how to govern and how to avoid being governed too much. Experimentation and transgressions of limits are vital in this critical ontology of ourselves, which he sees as a radical as opposed to a revolutionary approach, because it is practical and experimental in contrast to being abstract and ideological. Foucault's politics of critical engagement is antithetic to the nostalgias of reactionaries and revolutionaries alike, both of which are antithetic to democratic politics.*

Keywords: Ideology Critique; limits/transgression; normative theory; political critique; truth

Dyrberg, Torben Bech. *Foucault on the Politics of Parrhesia*. Basingstoke: Palgrave Macmillan, 2014.
DOI: 10.1057/9781137368355.0005.

Themes and challenges in Foucault's critical engagement

Foucault's attitude to critique is not only radical, but it is also distinctly political. By this I mean that it is not an approach like Critical Theory or Ideology Critique, which has political ramifications. It addresses head-on a number of fundamental topics in political theory/sociology/philosophy/science relating to how we understand power and political authority. It also shows that a Nietzsche inspired take on critique is practical, experimental and political instead of normative and judgemental. It is curious, it asks uncomfortable questions, it challenges what is facile and habitual and it confronts what we say with what we do. The later Foucault's way of reasoning about democracy and authority is, surprisingly perhaps, closer to Rawls and his notion of public reason than to Habermas' deliberative democracy. Like Rawls, he demonstrates how the negative view of political power precludes the possibility that a non-coercive political authority could occur, one which does *not* operate by thwarting the will/interests of others in its pursue of special interests. The point is that if one sticks to mainstream and so-called critical approaches – that power is a form of domination and politics entails conflict – then one will not be able to appreciate, let alone grasp, Foucault's reflections along the political authority/community axis, which leaves this opportunity open.

Foucault does two things. He shows his anti-essentialist and anti-functionalist way of conceptualizing power *and* he sets up what counts as democratic standards of interaction albeit somewhat implicitly. This is a normative political theory, but one that is considerably different compared to what we usually find in this genre, because it is political as opposed to be applied academic philosophical modelling. That is, he does not work out a moral argument from within a normative theory and then tries to apply it to politics. On the contrary, and this is particularly visible in his discussions of critique and *parrhesia*, he engages in political practice right from the start by working out his arguments in relation to political practice in general and political authorities and laypeople in particular.

Foucault's outline of the nature of critique, or rather how it operates, links up with his discussions of power. This is not surprising as he understands the condition of existence of critique in relation to a combination of how power relations function, where he focuses on authorities and their critics, and a libertarian and egalitarian gesture aiming to minimize traits of domination in exercises of power. The question is not so much *what* is critique, as to *how* it is practiced, that is, what happens when one engages in political critique? The latter obviously relies on the former in the sense that one has to know what one is looking for in the first place, but the point remains that the 'how' of practising critique is a key to understand the ways people react to being governed. Hence, there is a thematic similarity between Foucault's approach to critique and his earlier emphasis on the power/resistance couplet; one of the major differences being that he later on paid more explicit attention to the self as partaking in creating itself and its environment as opposed to being seen as a docile body, which at best could react to the power of productive submission.

The starting point for critique, says Foucault, is that people, for whatever reason, find a state of affair intolerable or unacceptable, or that they at any rate problematize how they are governed – what he refers to as 'voluntary insubordination' and 'reflected intractability', which are related to 'the politics of truth' (WC: 47). Problematization and reflection imply that individuals distance themselves from particular settings, meaning they are no longer caught by it in the sense of taken it for granted or seeing it as unavoidable. They might, however, still be bound by it; that is, they may be stuck in what Foucault called 'a state of domination', which cripples their faculties, their freedom of thought, and curtails their liberty to do what they conceive as acceptable options to act differently. Foucault's genealogical critique takes off from this distance and it challenges the limits which are imposed on us and which we impose on ourselves. To approach critique in this manner is political for at least five reasons.

First, the starting point is the differentiation acceptable/unacceptable or tolerable/intolerable, which is the bottom line for governing and hence for exercising political authority. This is a factual issue because people can accept regimes or ways of governing for a wide variety of reasons ranging from agreement and respect to fear of violent repression. This is opposed to issues concerning, for example, agreement, respect and legitimacy, which are imbued with theories of reason, obligation, ideology, and so forth.

Second, Foucault's take on critique is political as opposed to the epistemologically based counterparts in the Marxist tradition such as Critical Theory and Ideology Critique. His interest is not to unmask the truth beneath the surface of ideological distortions, but to focus on the axis of authority/laypeople including the problems of, and the reactions to, ways of governing people. The later Foucault's politics of critical engagement continues his earlier discussions of power/resistance by underlining that it is impossible to adopt an outsider position – a position which is, moreover, indulged by the nostalgias of reactionaries and revolutionaries alike, both of whom he views as antithetic to democratic politics: the one because it favours social hierarchies and obedience, the other because it is abstract and totalitarian.

Third, genealogical critique is practical because it deals more with what people do and how they act than with what they say and with their reasons and principles (Hoy 1998: 21). When we reflect on what we do and how we act, when we turn our doing and acting into objects of thought and thus detaches ourselves from it, it is because things have become uncertain, lost their familiarity or provoked difficulties.[1] It is the distance between the normal and the event that sparks off reflection upon what one is doing, with what one is or has become and how one comports oneself towards others. Thus reflection is freedom of thought, which leads to the next point.

Fourth, it concerns the experimental attitude of critique where practice is a test. In contrast to normative theories that measure the distance between actual norms and ideal norms according to a transcendental yardstick, Foucault sets out to 'confront what one is thinking and saying with what one is doing, with what one is' (PE: 374). This is another facet of distance, but this time the point is to minimize it to avoid a disjunction between ideas and life, words and deeds. In so doing, one cultivates one's ethos, which is an embodied freedom that links personal and political aspects of commonalty.

Fifth, to create or invent oneself revolves around becoming, which has two aspects. It is, as I said in the previous chapter, inseparable from power in the sense that it concerns the becoming of abilities to reflect, judge, decide, act and so on, all of which is a precondition for governing others. It is, moreover, both personal and public. The point is not to discover what we really are as private selves, but of questioning and possibly refusing what we have become. By transgressing limits, which position and identify us, the critical enterprise consists in desubjectivation, that is to say, to become different. This takes courage, which is a key theme in Foucault's discussion of *parrhesia*, and he refers to this personal *and* political challenge as the philosophical ethos of the critical ontology of ourselves. It is 'a historico-practical test of the limits that we may go beyond', and it is a 'work carried out by ourselves upon ourselves as free beings' (WE: 115). Curiosity, reflexivity, experimentation and courage are vital with regard to transgressing limits, and they pivot around and enrich individual freedom as a practical experience as opposed to being merely abstract and ideological.

Moral codes and ethical practices

To embark upon the practical and political aspects of critique, it will be pertinent to focus on the distance between morals and ethics. It is the distance between (1) the moral codes prescribing what is right and what is wrong and (2) the ways individuals actually live their lives in the light of these codes, which entice reflection and make critique possible (HS2: 25–30; see also Schirato et al. 2012: 182–8). There are two aspects of the code/practice typology. First, codes and practices can be seen as the poles in a continuum where the former is the sedimentation of the latter, that is, their formalization or the 'juridico-discursive representation' of practices. This implies, second, that moral codes are historically construed, and this means that the status ascribed to them as imperatives beyond questioning – whether universalistic or communitarian – cannot be upheld, but is open for critique. Both of these points politicize the field of investigation by asking to the historical structuring of the categories and the practices they order, which implies that one engages in negotiating or confronting them. This is the 'limit-attitude' where we have to be at the frontier, reflecting upon limits and transgressing them via practical critique which, according to Foucault, singles out the modern critical ethos (WE: 113–14). This mode of being does not take off from grand design of normative theory, but is rather an unfolding of an ethical and political perspective or commitment I choose to refer to as libertarian and egalitarian, which links individuality and commonalty, and sees neither of them as given a priori.

The critical ontology of ourselves probes the ethical formation of the self, challenges repressive modes of subjectivity and engages in creating new forms of subjectivity. Foucault does not see freedom as a foundational right of the subject for this reason. It is not only a practice that must be exercised; it is, more to the point, a vocation and an achievement, which is connected with its creative and agonistic nature of 'generating a power that is exercised over oneself so that one can be worthy of exercising it over others' (Mendieta 2011: 112; see also HOS: 97). This links up with the community aspect where Foucault asserts the becoming of a 'we' by confronting politics with problems it has to deal with, thereby transforming common frames of reference (PPP: 114–15). To approach the question of 'we' in this manner, Foucault counters two strands in modern identity politics: a communitarian and conservative insistence upon our cultural heritage ingrained in traditions and habits as a pre-political frame, on the one side, and a radical poststructuralist and realist contention asserting that the us/them enmity is the only or primary way to constitute the 'we'. It goes for both of them that the political imperative of demarcating the 'we' fits uneasily with modern pluralist democracy and is outright antithetic to the personal and political libertarian and egalitarian ethos characterizing the enlightenment attitude.

The couplet of moral code and ethical practice taps into frame of reference, tradition and identity, on the one hand, and experimentation, curiosity and becoming, on the other. This has implications for how one views individuality and commonalty, and it is, moreover, relevant for dealing with the analytical and political aspects at work in Foucault's critical enterprise, which are closely linked. The analytical aspect is ingrained in Foucault's problematization, which lays out the parameters of power, knowledge and ethics – alias rules governing action, delimitation of objects and relations to oneself – that define domains of enquiries. This involves an aspect of distance as, for example, questions concerning knowledge are dealt with in relation to power relations and ethics. Hence, distance refers to the broadening of the horizons of engagement, which goes hand in hand with questioning and relativizing established moral codes. It might better be described as 'a pathos of distance', which is a phrase Foucault inherits from Nietzsche, since problematization as the 'stepping outside of the alleged "shared values"' entices passion (Stone 2011: 150; see also Lemke 2012: 70). With the political aspect one makes the move from distance to risk by confronting prevailing norms, exposing hypocrisy and manipulation, practicing other forms of life, and so forth. This involves an element of danger, and thus also courage, as one is up against powerful interests or prevailing norms. This implies that one is exposed to various types of retaliations ranging from, say, public ridicule to state organized violence. This is a key issue in *parrhesia*, which I will deal with in the next chapter. Here it will suffice to say that the risky enterprise of engaging in critique involves not only a transformation of oneself, but also of the community, because it is bound up with the liberating act of asking questions, engaging in agonistic confrontations and negotiations, changing and pluralizing political allegiances and, accordingly, to take part in altering the rules of the political game and the moral codes.

Foucault's critique in contrast to Ideology Critique

Foucault's approach to critique differs as mentioned from Ideology Critique, which is epistemology-based just as it differs from the grand design of normative theories, which deduce 'the good society' from, for instance, an historical eschatology or a philosophical anthropology. Foucault's political line of enquiry, by contrast, looks at where to draw the line between how to govern and how to avoid being governed too much. The latter refers to criticizing being governed in this or that way according to this or that principle, which implies that critique is reflective and negotiated. Hence, critique orbits around power relations and forms of resistance seen in the light of the libertarian and egalitarian enlightenment ethos. It is essentially political as it proceeds along the authority/laypeople axis and aims to open up new avenues of political imagination, experimentation and practice as opposed to peeling off layers of manipulation in order to disclose 'the real thing'.

With Foucault's Nietzschean take on Critical Theory – his genealogical approach which 'has to fight the power-effects characteristic of any discourse that is regarded as scientific' and which 'brings into play the desubjugated knowledges' (SMD: 9, 11; see also TL: 81–7) – he turned against two adversaries: the System and Marxism. Against the former he asserted in the early/mid-1970s that bourgeois society was a generalized confinement – an assumption, which had political momentum at the time, and which was based on his analyses of prisons and his political work in GIP. The point was that the prison was the microcosm of society where anonymous bureaucratic surveillance would ensure, on the one hand, that individuals submitted to the rules and hence enrolled in the power relations of productive submission, and on the other, that societal order was maintained through disciplinary subjection, which would ensure normalization. He would, in line with Nietzsche, argue that the sublimation of cruelty in modern society – which would go under the names of civilization, progress, rationality, enlightenment and rights

– came with a price, namely that of a generalized disciplinary society in which individuals were turned into an economically efficient workforce whose political means to resist were curbed (Wolin 2010: 325). More specifically, he would argue that the juridico-discursive representation of power was an anachronistic straightjacket for political practice, because it forced it into a non-political scheme of dualisms such as those of order/disorder, peace/war, legitimacy/illegitimacy and consensus/conflict (PST: 139–41). Foucault held that 'discipline produces subjected and practised bodies, "docile" bodies. Discipline increases the forces of the body (in economic terms of utility) and diminishes these same forces (in political terms of obedience)' (DP: 138, see also 209, 218, 220–1; McNay 1994: 100–4). To argue on those lines Foucault seems close to a kind of inverse functionalism as the micro-physics of power would tend to become extrapolated to hold for society. This would confront his approach to power with a serious problem. Analytically, the problem was that the jump from local strategies at the micro level to general strategies at the macro level would render the ascending analysis of power superfluous and undercut the heterogeneity and unpredictability of power relations.[2] Politically, the problem was that it gave rise to an interpretation of Foucault's work as deterministic, which for all practical purposes eliminated the possibilities to resist modern power. Something on those lines seems to be the case when power becomes imbued with an economic functionality such as when 'the political anatomy of the body' formatted the rise of capitalism – that it was its political take-off.[3] No wonder that Poulantzas in *State, Power, Socialism* from 1978 (65–9, 77–81) on the whole endorsed this line of argument as it sustained what he thought was a material underpinning of ideology operating in what Althusser had dubbed 'the ideological state apparatuses'.

In addition, Foucault staunchly rejected that modern Western society was democratic. 'It is only too clear', he said in his debate with Chomsky on Dutch television in November 1971,[4] 'that we are living under a regime of a dictatorship of class, of a power of class which imposes itself by violence, even when the instruments of this violence are institutional and constitutional.' The point then was to 'criticize and attack' what at first would appear as politically neutral institutions 'in such a manner that the political violence which has always exercised itself obscurely through them will be unmasked, so that one can fight against them' (HN: 41) This type of criticism aimed at unmasking the class enemy and its means of manipulation to get people to comply is especially clear in his analyses of the model of sovereignty with its judicially codified liberty and equality. The point was that theoretical and legal abstractions obscure the concrete and practical effects of power mechanisms in general and disciplinary techniques of productive submission in particular (Wolin 2010: 311–12). An elaborated system of rights could thus go hand in hand with a no less sophisticated system of surveillance and normalization, which implied that what 'enabled sovereignty to be democratised ... was fundamentally determined by and grounded in mechanisms of disciplinary coercion' (TL: 105). The problem is not that discipline as productive submission facilitates efficiency and hierarchical authorities while also making it possible to institutionalize an egalitarian democratic set-up of popular sovereignty. It is rather that Foucault in this way of arguing came close to what he was otherwise highly critical of, namely a critique of ideology position in which libertarian and egalitarian rhetoric covers over *de facto* domination working in-depth of society. This rhetoric is thus presented as the surface manifestation sugar-coating disciplinary coercion, which is the real stuff making up 'the political anatomy' of the body and underpinning 'capillary' domination, that is, the micro-physics of power.

The other adversary was that of Marxism. Foucault's critical approach differed from a Marxist one according to which the varied forms of domination in modern society could, in the last instance, be referred back to the existence of social classes pivoting around economic exploitation, although he did himself, occasionally, explain things in this way as the above quote indicates. He was also critical of the high level of abstraction of laws of history, the logic of capital, capital/labour relationships and so on, all of which licensed speculative intellectual deductions or descending types of analysis, as he would also call it. The problem with deductions was that '[t]hey are essentially too facile, because we can say precisely the opposite', that is, 'I think that we can deduce whatever we like from the general phenomenon of the domination of the bourgeois class' (SMD: 32–3; see also TL: 99–101; Smart 1983: 83–4). A genealogical critique would have to proceed the other way around by showing how mechanisms of exclusion, control, surveillance and normalization turned out to 'reveal their political usefulness and to lend themselves to economic profit' to become 'colonised and maintained by global mechanisms and the entire State system' (TL: 101). This type of criticism of the Marxist set-up also made him sceptical of notions of ideology, which he found problematic for a number of reasons.

In the first place the notion of ideology insulated consciousness from being by treating the former as a superstructure, which was in the last instance determined by the base. It assumed in other words that 'ideology stands in a secondary position relative to something which functions as its infrastructure, as its material, economic determinant' (TP: 118). This way of looking at consciousness and ideology was problematic because it was a rerun of the subject/object dualism, which was idealistic, partly because it defied the materiality of consciousness as something that was formed historically and hence susceptible to a genealogical analytics, and partly because it was, as I mentioned above, already a product of discourse, that is, the articulation of power and knowledge. It follows that the notion of ideology was difficult because it referred to a subject (BP: 58; Racevskis 1983: 93).

In Marxism it was the bourgeoisie as the manipulating subject that vis-à-vis the delusionary mechanisms of capitalism induced false consciousness in the working class, which was, accordingly, the manipulated subject. By the same token he was critical of seeing the latter as the powerless class, which enjoyed the privilege of embodying the emancipatory vision of eliminating class society and thus political power and domination. This type of criticism was only natural given, partly, Foucault's assertion (SMD: 29) that 'power is not something that is divided between those who have it and hold it exclusively, and those who do not have it and are subject to it', and partly his inclination to see the 'will to power' as the bottom line of every historical construct and as something far exceeding the question of class. He saw the disciplinary forms of power operating in all sorts of institutions as supporting and even conditioning class power (HN: 41).[5] More generally, Foucault's genealogy was directed against philosophies of the subject as his point was to study 'the constitution of the subject across history which has led us up to the modern concept of the self' (ST: 151; see also THS: 186). His later reflections on the historical ontology of ourselves in relation to power, knowledge and ethics further interrogated the political being of the self, which was at the same time a politicization of Kant's critique.[6]

Foucault's distaste for ideology had also to do with its reliance upon the distinction between true knowledge and science, on the one hand, and false knowledge, prejudice and the like, on the other. Two points should be noted here. First, he did not, needless to say, set out to uncover the truth of human nature behind layers of alienation and false consciousness. Because he did not assume there was an authentic primal matter that could be excavated and emancipated.⁷ So, instead of assuming that there was something hidden, which ought to be liberated, he asked how it could be that we attempt to decode the innermost secrets about ourselves in the name of truth be that in science or in confession (OP: 107; Rajchman 1985: 89, 92). Later on he focused on how these attempts linked up with the invention and deployment of governmental rationalities, technologies and mentalities. There was not then any attempt to go behind the discursive field to get at 'reality' by trying to bring forth what had so far remained alienated. The ethos of transgression that carries this form of critique does not operate with an either/or alternative of being for or against, inside or outside (HS1: 94–6; 1984: 43, 45–6). This is so because transgression is situated within the political field and, more fundamentally, because Foucault's argument is not an epistemological one geared to unmasking what is true or real beneath or behind layers of manipulation, but a political one geared to understanding the workings of governmental authorities and how people react to being governed. This is especially clear in his later works, but, as I have already argued, it was also his concern from the very beginning although it would seem that he did not have the language to address it comprehensively and explicitly.

Yet another aspect of Foucault's disapproval of ideology, which is seldom raised in relation to this issue, has to do with his critique of totalizing and universalizing conceptions of social/political interaction, society and so forth. Ideology for him would connote not only a forged or facile type of explanation, something which could explain everything and hence nothing; it would also be artificial in the sense that people would have to conform to a master plan envisioned and carried out by a political elite. This was, as he mentioned on several occasions, extremely dangerous and had led to disasters, as it had to rely on the use of systematic violence on a massive scale.⁸

Seen from Foucault's political point of view it did not make sense to speak of a unifying and underlying law of history, which was there to be discovered by science. The reason was that truth and power were two sides of the same coin, which, from the viewpoint of Ideology Critique, would undercut the possibility of critique and hence resistance. However, this does not have to be the case, and this is the second point, which is particularly important for the argument I am pursuing here, because it, once again, suggests a political, as opposed to an epistemological, reading of his undertaking. The critical epistemological reading of Foucault's approach to the relationship of power and truth has been inclined to assert that he was a relativist as the truth was what counted as true by the dominant discourses. In other words, truth is what the powerful say it is. This is so because Foucault, in the eyes of Habermas, Fraser and Taylor, for instance, does not have a normative theory, which can provide a solid – and that means pre-political – foundation for evaluating political practice, which is, of course, true.[9] To approach critique in this manner is, in my opinion, off target, as it does not focus on Foucault's political take on critique, truth and self-reflection, which becomes even more obvious when seen in light of his later discussions of critique and *parrhesia*.

The political angle is, however, already clear in, for example, 'Truth and Power' from 1977 where Foucault speaks of the politics of truth, which can be seen as implicitly addressed to a Critical Theory or Critique of Ideology type of argument. Foucault does not focus on 'the ensemble of truths which are to be discovered and accepted', but is concerned rather with the battle 'around truth'. He is referring to 'the ensemble of rules according to which the true and the false are separated and specific effects of power attached to the true' and 'how effects of truth are produced within discourses'.[10] In addition to the political as opposed to the epistemological reading of truth, it is important to note that when Foucault speaks of power/knowledge he is thinking of those forms of knowledge, which are 'invested in complex institutional systems' governing modern life. As he goes on explaining, 'I undertook the analysis of a knowledge whose visible body is not theoretical or scientific discourse, nor literature either, but a regulated, everyday practice.'[11] These two remarks – the battle around truth concerned with setting the rules and the specific type of knowledge Foucault is looking at – should make it clear that the issue he is grappling with has nothing to do with the epistemological one of delusion vs clarity.

The issue at hand is not that of the manipulated consensus of self-imposed coercion associated with false as opposed to true consciousness where consensus is rational and autonomous as it is based on what Habermas refers to as the peculiar force of the better argument's absence of force. According to him, for criticism to be valid it *must* be based on the *belief* of universal standards concerning rational discourse – standards delineating an ideal dialogue that serves as 'a transcendental presupposition of actual dialogues' and, accordingly, as the truth condition measuring the nature and scope of ideological distortions of actual consensus (Hoy 1979: 93; see also Rajchman 1985: 78–9). This 'must' and this 'belief' both refer to Habermas' elusive authority, which presents itself as an extra-political and inter-subjectively valid standard, which trumps political disagreement. For Foucault, by contrast, Habermas' 'utopia of completely transparent communication' (ESF: 298) is not able to break free of a negative view of power relations. Moreover, basically, Foucault's exploration of 'regulated, everyday practice' and his way of approaching truth in relation to power and knowledge is directly concerned with how to govern. That is, it is a question of how political authority is exercised.

Foucault is neither concerned with true/false nor with consensus/conflict. This is so because critique does not take upon itself the task of judging whether X is more true or morally better than Y, because the point is not, as Owen says (2002: 227), that of 'correcting an ideological mistake' but of 'freeing a person from the limitations of a picture and of presenting another one'. Moreover, the reason that Foucault launches a political argument in which the truth/falsity of agents' beliefs belongs to the realm of what Rawls terms 'comprehensive doctrines'. This is particularly clear in Habermas' validity claim, which means that a democratic political authority should not deal with it as it can only be settled politically by coercive means. This might be the reason Foucault claims: 'It is not a matter of emancipating truth from every system of power ... But of detaching the power of truth from the forms of hegemony ... within which it operates at the present time.'[12] The point is not to rescue an epistemological truth from a political one, thus ascertaining the authority of the former from the falsity of the latter. Instead, the point is a political one of being able to criticize existing forms of political authorities and their claim to speak the truth and define what counts as necessary policies. The issue is, in other words, that of either accepting or not accepting what political authorities say and do.

Notes

1   PPP: 117. In a manner that recalls Heidegger's argument that thinking is the process of turning that which was at hand into an object, which is sparked-off when they break down, Foucault mentions in his lecture on Nietzsche (WK: 210): 'To say that there is no knowledge in itself is to say that the subject-object relation ... is not the foundation of knowledge but is in reality produced by it.'

2. This jump from micro to macro was part of the reason Ernesto Laclau expressed reservations against Foucault's approach to power, as he saw it as indicative of the absence of an hegemonic logic in his argument (seminar at Essex University 1987). See also McNay 1994: 104; Jessop 1987: 78.
3. DP: 136–8, 164, 220–3; 1980a: 88–9. For references to thematic links between Foucault's argument and Weber's protestant ethics as facilitating the rise of capitalism: see, for example, Dean 1994: ch. 4; Gordon 1987; O'Neill 1987; Smart 1983: ch. 6.
4. HN: 39. This is Foucault at his most revolutionary leftist mood speaking among other things of the proletariat's need to exercise 'a violent, dictatorial, and even bloody power' (HN: 52) over its class enemy and vehemently rejecting empty phrases of responsibility and justice, because '[o]ne makes war to win, not because it's just' (HN: 51). For an amusing description of the encounters between Foucault, Chomsky and Elders, who was an anarchist hosting the programme, see Miller 1994: 200–3.
5. See also SMD: 15–17. The theme of supplementary power is found in Foucault's analyses of sovereignty and discipline where contract/oppression, in which power is regulated by law, is supplemented by war/repression in which productive and disciplinary power produces normalization. See also HS1: 99–100 where he speaks of the 'Rule of double conditioning' between local and general strategies and that power relations are 'intentional and non-subjective', which means that they cannot be the property of subjects as they partake in shaping them. For an illustrating discussion of the latter, see Lynch 2011: 22–3 and Hook 2007: 81–4.
6. WC: 113ff. Elsewhere Foucault shortly outlines 'the two great traditions which have divided modern philosophy' founded by Kant. On the one hand we have Anglo-Saxon analytical philosophy, 'which posed the question of the conditions of possibility of a true knowledge', and on the other, we find the tradition which Foucault is steeped in, which deals with another type of questioning that involves 'an ontology of the present, of present reality, an ontology of modernity, an ontology of ourselves' (GSO: 20–1).
7. NGH: 153; PST: 138; HN: 5–7, 43–4. This does not imply that it is futile to unmask what passes as common sense or what is taken for granted. The point is that this is a political task as opposed to epistemological one, because it is geared to take action and change the ways we conduct ourselves and others.
8. Foucault dealt with this way of criticizing ideology in the late 1970s, which in part at least was influenced by the publication of Solzhenitsyn's *The Gulag Archipelago* as well as the new philosophers and their critique of Marxism.
9. Fraser 1981: 275–6, 282–6. See also the debate between Patton (1989) and Taylor (1989). In addition, see also Owen 2002: 224–6.

10 TP: 132, 118. See also ESF: 296 in which he stresses, 'I am absolutely not saying that games of truth are just concealed power relations – that would be a horrible exaggeration.' See also Dews 1986: 81; May 1993: 100.
11 CP: 5–6. Foucault's text stems from the pamphlet he wrote when applying for a chair in philosophy at the Collège de France in which he 'presented the logic behind his research'. See also Eribon 1991: 214. The point is, as Foucault says elsewhere (TJF: 2), 'how social practices may engender domains of knowledge'.
12 TP: 133. For a similar argument but seen in relation to knowledge and science, see AK: 185–6. See also Racevskis 1983: 81–4.

4
The Politics of Critique: Political Engagement and Government

Abstract: *Foucault's view of power as a creative capacity has three implications for how critique is conceived. He outlines an anti-essentialist and anti-functionalist way of conceptualizing power and resistance; he specifies the criteria for political interaction as autonomous and on this basis he discusses what counts as democratic standards of interaction. By launching his argument from within the political field of agonistic forces, in contrast to applying normative theory to politics, Foucault is able to situate political ethics in realpolitik. Thus conceived critique and* parrhesia *manage to connect three axes of importance for grasping the specificity of political practice, which complement or even summarize his work on power, knowledge and ethics by giving them a distinctively political turn.*

Keywords: enlightenment; freedom; Kant; limit/transgression; Marxism; ontology of ourselves; political critique; radical/revolutionary

Dyrberg, Torben Bech. *Foucault on the Politics of Parrhesia.* Basingstoke: Palgrave Macmillan, 2014. DOI: 10.1057/9781137368355.0006.

The post-politics context

For the post-trends taking off in the 1980s, it was not Foucault's 'liberal freedoms' that caught the eye; nor was it his Kantian and Nietzschean inspired discussions of critique, his elaboration of power/domination vis-à-vis agonistic encounters or his discussions of power, knowledge and ethics in relation to governmentality. Taken on board, above all, by the critical, radical or leftist establishment were his arguments about the inseparable links of power/knowledge and power/resistance. The reason might be that this was the easy way out of the *cul-de-sac* of Marxist critique in general and Ideology Critique in particular. That is, one did not have to revise one's basic political instincts about the repressive system; all that was needed was to turn the epistemology handle 180 degrees from objectivism to relativism and then re-launch Ideology Critique in the new jargon of post-everything. Power/knowledge and power/resistance offered a new opportunity to stay radical whilst at the same time criticizing or deconstructing everything that smacked of essentialism, objectivity and universalism – the new buzzwords of criticism. These dualisms made it possible to nurture one's oppositional identity by turning the earlier modernist radicalism upside-down. The Marxists' insistence on the laws of history with their irreversible development and progress as well as the grandiose schemes of emancipation ending history were suffocated in the 1980s in the wake of political fatigue and defeatism. Mainstream concepts of the constitutive subject, truth, justice, freedom and rationality went down the drain too as all of it, according to the new trend, turned out to be ambiguous, everything had ignoble origins contaminated by power, which could be unmasked and deconstructed *ad infinitum* as there were suddenly no longer an Archimedean point to hold on to (NGH: 143–8).

Instead, we were presented with a circular and relativist storytelling according to which there was nothing but context and where one form of repression was replaced by another, because everything at the end of the day boiled down to power struggles: who got the upper hand and who was the underdog, what was in and what was out, and so forth. This was Nietzsche's 'endlessly repeated play of domination', the only difference being that this time no one had the fantasy, let alone the desire, to break out of this vicious circle. Within just a few years a leftist common sense had changed drastically from lofty eschatological vanguard visions of socialist revolution heralding the end of power politics to what would appear as the much more realistic scenario that any type of political order, even a democratic one, could only be thought of as a way of organizing hierarchy and domination as power could not be done away with. This could be read as a sobering up or an acknowledgement of political realities, which it no doubt was; yet, it turned things upside-down as it was still under the spell of the two most persistent axioms of modern political theory. Power was still repressive and its vehicles were still conflicts of vested interests now supplemented with the identity politics of all kinds of subaltern groups.

What is at issue here is the paradox that just about the only thing that did not get caught up in the post-modern grinding machine was the deep-seated premises of mainstream political science, political sociology, political philosophy and so on, as well as Marxism, that power is domination in one way or the other and that politics is conflict either covert or open. The otherwise radically minded post-trends simply took over these axioms, as they seemed to fit nicely with a phony hard-boiled cynicism, which was more likely a façade behind which lurked a melancholic political mood paired with a lack of will to revise old intellectual habits. Now, it was no longer a matter of uncovering the truth and getting the values right as in the old days of Ideology Critique, just a few years earlier, but of unmasking every value as hypocrisy, that is, a cynical cover-up for political strategies, interests and conspiracies. For the radical power/resistance identity politics associated with the never aging new social movements, this implied that political power struggles were seen as an authentic existential condition in contrast to consensus, which was depoliticized and sedimented domination. Hence the glorification of the political as the root cause of everything, which leftist scholars took over from Carl Schmitt (Dyrberg 2009). But opposite the radical right, which was on the move, the academic left had not much on offer with the result that it isolated itself and indulged in hate politics. This kind of anti-politics says more about the leftist post-trends than of Foucault and it shows how necessary it is to clarify that Foucault's *political* argument leads in a very different direction.

How to govern and how to avoid being governed

Foucault's later work, particularly the posthumous published lectures, spell out more clearly and systematically than did his earlier texts that politics does not depend upon conflict/consensus and that power is not just productive repression but also unpredictable, empowering, facilitating and so forth. I will now turn to this as it shows that it is unviable to interpret Foucault from the vantage point of the old power/resistance matrix with which he has largely been identified as it suits a leftist radical self-image – the vanguard mentality of seeing through ideological distortions and to be against the system no matter what one then approves of. For those doing Ideology Critique, to be radical means to have objective knowledge of the system and not being caught up by the system. Many Foucauldians would go for the former and readily acknowledge their fate of being caught up. By contrast, the late Foucault provides new insights as to what it means to be radical and critical, which is part and parcel of his elaboration and systematization of *political* categories of analysis and which, again, are vital for democratic governmentality.

Despite the fact that both types of critique aim to expose that which we take for granted or self-evident, should not, in fact, be accepted as such, and although both engage in or proceed by way of self-reflection, which means that both of them are lodged in the enlightenment tradition, there are, nonetheless, marked differences between them. Foucault aims to capture these differences by referring to two trends in the enlightenment tradition concerning truth: the dominant one associated with an 'analytics of truth', which is geared towards epistemology, and the other one of a 'history of truth', which is geared to political ethics and is more akin to Foucault's own undertaking. Whilst the former focuses on the conditions and limits to the subject's access to truth, which is what informs modern philosophy from Descartes onwards, the latter investigates what enables the subject to have access to the truth, that is, what must the subject be like to be speaking truthfully (Stone 2011: 145)? Basically, this alternative boils down to the nature of their undertakings as an epistemologically and politically based critique, respectively, which has several consequences with regard to how a critical approach proceeds, which is illustrated in Table 4.1.

Foucault's *political* critique is inspired by the Kantian ethos of the enlightenment, which is centred on the quest for autonomy and the courage it takes to know, on the one hand, and Nietzschean perspectivism, centred on contingency and struggle, on the other, differs considerably from Ideology Critique. For the latter, as we have seen, the point was to break through layers of manipulating class interests, which alienated the oppressed subjects from their real selves,

TABLE 4.1 *Contrasting Critical Theory/Ideology Critique and Foucault's political critique*

Critique	Critical Theory/Ideology Critique	Foucault's critique
Type	Epistemological	Political
Basis	Abstract knowledge	Practical power/knowledge
Code	Truth vs manipulation	Acceptance vs non-acceptance
Engagement	Eschatological and utopian	Limits and transgressions
Social agents	Collective: social classes	Individuals acting politically
Procedure	Deduction	Investigative
Approach	Abstract and law-like	Practical and historical
Order	Given pre-politically	Created politically
Perspective	God's eye view: wannabe objectivism	Contextual: political authorities and their critics
Politics	Outside-in: revolutionary or conservative	Inside-out: radical and experimental
Ethics	Truth telling vs lying Good vs bad	Appropriate vs inappropriate Efficient vs inefficient
Political agents	The intellectual political vanguard or the ruling class	Political authorities and their critics

pinpointed their objective interests, or at least their real interests, and elucidated their epochal mission of putting an end to exploitation. In this move from appearance to essence via raising class consciousness, truth and politics were welded together. The premise was that when the oppressed masses via learning processes of self-reflection threw away 'the veil of ignorance' they would see clearly and thus become enlightened, and due to this very fact they would release themselves from their self-imposed captivity and resist exploitation. In contrast to this rationalist and basically non-political form of emancipation, which is in any case out of touch with political realities,[1] Foucault's *political* critique is an attitude and a way of conducting oneself as opposed to a type of knowledge which pretends to have a privileged access to the truth. Contrary to the Critical Theory tradition, truth and authority are not opposed to each other by definition and it is not, in any case, the task of political authorities to take sides in matters of science or comprehensive doctrines. What matters politically – and this is what critique is about for Foucault – is 'a voluntary choice' to cultivate an attitude that is able to grasp the modern condition 'that at one and the same time marks a relation of belonging and presents itself as a task' (WE: 105). Political critique is a virtue that is bound up with being modern. It is not only to take care of oneself, but also to make a virtue of necessity, as it were, that is, to cope with modern conditions of life, which Foucault, quoting Baudelaire, refers to as 'the ephemeral, the fleeting, the contingent' (WE: 105). In Foucault's reading of Kant and Baudelaire, the modern attitude is not, then, contemplative but is an ongoing encounter with one's conditions, which are at once a collective process and an individual challenge. It 'is an exercise in which extreme attention to what is real is confronted with the practice of a liberty that simultaneously respects this reality and violates it' (WE: 108, see also 101–2).

The exercise and the practice Foucault speaks of here is the opposite of the search for authenticity, which comes in all sorts of shapes. Today, it is often associated with nationalist, religious and culturalist revivals and adorned by many strands of the left as a way of asserting what radical politics means – typically expressed in a communitarian and anti-imperialist/West position. In contrast, the modern attitude is based on an assumption 'that the self is not given to us' and this implies that 'we have to create ourselves as a work of art'.[2] This is a heroic task inasmuch as the individual voluntarily puts itself at stake by resisting established truths, habits and injustices committed by powerful persons – all of which depends on personal integrity, courage and sound judgement.[3] But although it is heroic, it is not a prerogative for the select few, that is, it is not an elitist recipe for how to live the good life or for how to do politics.

It is no surprise then that Foucault was sceptical, if not outright hostile, towards ambitions of uniting objectivity and emancipation alias truth and politics, which in fact end up assigning a subordinate status to the political power of authority and critique. His earlier discussions of truth-seeking knowledge, which went hand in hand with disciplinary apparatuses of surveillance and normalization, indicate the authoritarian danger of this endeavour. The same goes for his more sketchy remarks on socialist regimes, which have not 'managed to function without a more-or-less developed Gulag system'.[4] In both cases, Foucault's critical concern, which also marks the significance of his power analytics, is to disclose two things.

First, that when political thought and practice are confined by the model of sovereignty, we become unable to grasp how other types of domination, such as disciplinary normalization regulate behaviour and has a political impact. It is here we find Foucault's discussions of the co-existence of the two incommensurable forms of power, namely that extending liberties and rights democratized sovereignty and that this went hand in hand with surveillance, control and normalization. The problem for an emancipatory politics was that whilst it would push for more rights it had no eye for the repressive aspects of discipline and biopolitics. Second, that critique instead of focusing on true/false should be a matter of opening up political possibilities by paying 'extreme attention' to what conditions us in order to show that our sense of political agency has been crippled (Owen 2002: 223). Critique is here levelled against 'the consequences of the state of domination caused by an unjustified political situation' and the 'truth game' it plays is that of 'pointing out that there are other reasonable options, by teaching people what they don't know about their own situation, their working conditions, and their exploitation'.[5] Falzon (1998: 88) argues similarly that 'resistance to domination does not presuppose the normative ideal of a true discourse, in which difference and conflict will be overcome and we will formulate our organizing principles in a collective, consensual voice. It is rather the expression of other voices, new voices'. Both these aspects of critique require shifting focus from viewing politics *outside-in* as in the objectivist synthesis of truth and politics associated with Critical Theory to seeing politics *inside-out* by focusing on the political axis of authorities/laypeople and the critics of being governed in this or that way. This perspective on political critique and, by extension, public political reasoning, stresses that it is an interactional principle that is not governed by other logics than a political one, and that it deals with the practical stuff of behaviour and acting, which is both personal and political.

It goes for Foucault's political approach, in contrast to the Ideology Critique position, that critique and authority are two sides of the same coin. There are two points, which are important to deal with when setting out to elaborate a distinctively political way of conceptualizing critique/authority. Negatively, it is to ward off those ways of categorizing politics, which are grounded in *social* interaction and which, accordingly, see politics in derivative terms. Positively, it is to elaborate what specifically characterizes *political* interaction and hence to see public political reasoning as 'freestanding' as Rawls would say. Here it is significant that Foucault's argument revolved more and more explicitly around the political power of authority, which he addressed in terms of 'the question of government' that sets out 'to structure the possible field of action of others'. This is a transformative or creative capacity that is 'neither warlike nor juridical', which means that it is neither modelled on violence or struggle nor on 'voluntary linking' (SP: 221; see also DP: 28). This argument captures the specificity and autonomy of political practice in a nutshell and illustrates the anti-political inclination of the conflict/consensus approach in which the political is unthinkable without conflicting interests whereas the social is defined as the residual category of consensus.

Political authorities have to cope with risks and possibilities, deciding what to do when and how, organize, guide, regulate and control all sorts of events, trends, relations and so on in the most appropriate and efficient manner. Regardless of whether this governing is seen as oppressive or empowering, the other side of the coin is how laypeople try to avoid being governed in this or that way, on the basis of this or that principle or goal, which inflicts certain costs on people, which is also a matter of coping with risks and possibilities. The first characterization of critique is then, says Foucault (WC: 45, 75), 'the art of not being governed like that and at that cost'; and, he adds on later, 'the will not to be governed is always the will not to be governed thusly, like that, by these people, at this price'. It should be clear that critique is a form of resistance, which is geared to the relation between those who govern and those who are governed, that is, the political authority relation, which concerns the practices and reasons for governing in this or that way (Oksala 2007: 86–7).

Critique is not just a matter of being oppositional and rejecting being governed because there is no position outside the network of power relations. There is, says Foucault (HS1: 96–7) 'no single locus of great Refusal, no soul of revolt, source of all rebellions or pure law of the revolutionary', just as there is not 'an originary freedom, absolutely and wholeheartedly resistant to any governmentalization' (WC: 75). Instead of being 'a demolition job, one of rejection or refusal', criticism is rather an investigative job, a reflexive and negotiated type of act, and an integral part of the political authority relation, which 'consists of analysing and reflecting upon limits' (OP: 107; WE: 113). To approach critique in this way is different from Foucault's earlier anarchic figure of resistance and counter-identity against the system according to which those who resisted were outside and marginalized. Now, by contrast, he engages in what he terms a critical ontology of ourselves, which falls squarely in-between descriptive and prescriptive genres. It is absorbed in historical facts of how we are made subjects and hostile to providing normative foundations or criteria for critique *and* it is motivated by and geared to a critical engagement of disrupting conformity and 'states of domination' marked by hierarchy and obedience.

The politics of critical engagement

Foucault's central concern is, in the words of Norris (1994: 169), 'to articulate an ethics premised on the values of autonomy, freedom, and self-determination attained through an exercise of practical will'. I have already mentioned some of the key features of this concern. It seeks to create ourselves instead of searching for our authentic self; it is practical and experimental in contrast to being contemplative; it favours an ethos of perpetual transformation as opposed to faithfulness to doctrines; and it is historical and practical rather than transcendental and abstract. In addition, whilst it is geared to dealing with the event and the singular, it is also committed to building a sense of democratic political community in which truthfulness and trustworthiness are political virtues. All of this implies that this political ethics is more concerned with getting the facts right, thus understanding our historical context and how it conditions the way things are done than with construing universally valid norms from which we can deduce what is right and wrong. No such deduction is possible in Foucault's argument, because everything can be deduced from abstract ideological assumptions and because of the totalitarian danger of setting up normative straightjackets.

In order to look into Foucault's politics of critical engagement, I will deal with two closely linked issues both of which revolve around his approach to limits and their transgression, which is important for understanding his way of approaching the politics of critique. The first one picks up the discussion concerning archaeological and genealogical aspects of practices of freedom. These are situated in the tension accentuated by modernity between attending to the conditions that mark one's reality and belonging, on the one hand, and the heroic or courageous acts where one dares to make use of one's reason to challenge this reality of established customs, truths and moral codes, thus putting oneself at risk, on the other. This is the critical ontology of ourselves, which is related to the second issue. It concerns Foucault's short mentioning of the contrast between revolutionary and radical approaches to constituting the regulation of public authorities by law in the late eighteenth and the early nineteenth centuries. These issues are, above all, interesting because they flesh out what it means to look at politics inside-out and highlight that a radical as opposed to a revolutionary take on critique is one that is guided by a practical and experimental attitude and goes for partial transformations (WE: 114; see also Patton 2005: 280–2). Both these aspects are essential for discussing *parrhesia* and public political reasoning, which is also to say that they are essential for modern democracy.

With the critical ontology of ourselves, of which Foucault speaks in his discussions of the enlightenment, critique and freedom, he picks up a theme he dealt with in the early 1960s, namely that of limit and transgression. This is an obvious move considering, first, that nothing is given least of all in modern society, which is, as mentioned, ephemeral, fleeting and contingent, and where we have to invent ourselves; and second, that critique is not a matter of rejection or refusal as there is no Archimedean point from where such a demolition job could take off. Instead, the critical encounter, attitude or ethos is a 'limit-experience' or 'limit-attitude' – at once here and beyond. 'We have', Foucault goes on (WE: 113), 'to move beyond the outside-inside alternative, we have to be at the frontiers. Criticism indeed consists of *analyzing and reflecting upon limits*'. This is to be understood in relation to partly his general relationalist approach, which stands as a critique of essentialism and foundationalism, and partly his discussion of Kant.

Foucault's treatment of Kant is especially interesting in this context. He scrutinizes Kant's text on the enlightenment and his attempt to set-up strict limits between the public use of reason where freedom reigns, and the private use of reason, which is restricted and obedience reigns.[6] In analysing and reflecting upon limits, Foucault radicalizes Kant by looking into how we are conditioned historically in order 'to transform the critique conducted in the form of necessary limitation into a practical critique that takes the form of a possible transgression' (WE: 113). In doing so, the critical task is to seek beyond these limits, to 'separate out, from the contingency that has made us what we are, the possibility of no longer being, doing, or thinking what we are, do, or think' (WE: 114). Critique involves in other words 'desubjectivation'. This is another way of praising an experimental attitude where curiosity, generosity and courage give way for new possibilities and risks all of which contribute to shaping new subjectivities that offer more space for autonomy and ethical self-formation (Lemke 2012: 71). This is an art of creation, where we engage ourselves practically and experimentally, we work on our limits, which is 'a patient labor giving form to our impatience for liberty' and thus take part in 'the undefined work of freedom' (WE: 119, 114).

Freedom is undefined for at least three reasons, which have to do with openness – and openness for Foucault means, above all, to be sceptical of necessary limitations, normative foundations and value judgements, not to mention the Grand theory tradition of universalizing and totalizing visions of emancipation associated with Marxism.[7] Freedom is undefined, first, because it is formulated negatively in line with Kant for whom *Aufklärung* is defined as *Ausgang*,[8] which is clear in the above quotes related to desubjectivation of 'not being governed like that' and 'no longer being, doing, or thinking'. This means that it seeks to go beyond certain ways of governing inasmuch as they are seen as abusive or crippling our capacities to govern ourselves and others. However, in line with the liberal tradition of negative liberty it does not set a goal to be pursued or criteria to follow in order to ensure to be on the right track as it were. Second, freedom is an art described in terms of invention and creation, which means that it is not conceived as an implementation of a ready-made idea, but as something singular. Similarly, Foucault is adamant to point out that freedom/liberty can never be assured simply by a constitutional set-up or by institutions in general, because it only exists by being exercised and having an impact (SKP: 245). This has both individual and collective aspects by stressing that liberty is no stronger than the actual will to defend it and that this defence might lead to new forms of rights (Patton 2005: 275–84). Third, freedom is a possibility not only by pointing beyond the existing order of things, but also in the more specific sense of focusing on 'the acquisition of capabilities and the struggle for freedom', which have characterized Western societies. The point is to raise the stakes of the enlightenment ethos: of how 'the growth of capabilities' can be 'disconnected from the intensification of power relations', which Foucault identifies with the strategies of domination associated with discipline and normalization.[9]

There are two closely connected aspects in relation to critique and freedom, which have an affinity to archaeological and genealogical investigations, respectively. First, one has to look at the nature of the rules and habits, assumptions and prescriptions, on which accepted and institutionalized practices are based. In this investigation of specific historical conditions, one has to look at 'what type of assumptions, of familiar notions, of established, unexamined ways of thinking the accepted practices are based' (IT: 456). What we get with this archaeological method is the delineation of an historical *a priori* that conditions the configuration and regulation of knowledge in a particular context and in a certain period, and hence the ways in which relations of power/knowledge are structured in institutions. This method is not an epistemological effort to lay down criteria for rationality, objectivity and progress, nor does it look at 'what is true or false, founded or unfounded, real or illusory, scientific or ideological, legitimate or abusive'. Instead, it seeks to 'discover the discursive, the institutional and the social practices from which these sciences arose' (WC: 59; ST: 152). The point is 'that criticism is no longer going to be practiced in the search for formal structures with universal value, but rather as an historical investigation into the events that have led us to constitute ourselves and to recognize ourselves as subjects of what we are doing, thinking, saying' (WE: 113; see also Patton 2003: 521). This is also, in part at least, an answer to those who criticize Foucault for not construing a normative ground from which critique can take off. His point is not to take a stance as to what is legitimate and what is not, but to go into what frames discourses as well as 'to analysing critically how power becomes accepted as legitimate/illegitimate' (Jenkins 2011: 170).

Second, one has to show how that which appears natural, self-evident or common sense 'will no longer be accepted as such. Practicing criticism is a matter of making facile gestures difficult' (PC: 155; see also Foucault in Goldstein 1991: 12). For the same reason, this practice is an emancipatory politics of sorts, neither abstract nor utopian but practical and aimed at the political ramifications of everyday life. This is a call for constantly questioning and challenging the normal state of affairs, 'showing that things are not as obvious as people believe, making it so that what is taken for granted is no longer taken for granted. To do criticism is to make harder those acts which are now too easy'.[10] Critique as a thoughtful activity creates a distance, it problematizes and objectifies; it is a distancing from types of actions and behaviour, which makes them lose their familiarity. 'Thought is freedom in relation to what one does', says Foucault (PPP: 388), 'the motion by which one detaches oneself from it, establishes it as an object, and reflects on it as a problem.' This creates room for curiosity – understood as 'that which enables one to get free of oneself'[11] – and freedom for thought and action to experiment with other possibilities and evaluating these. Curiosity and freedom are two sides of the same coin, which politicize existing conditions by questioning and disrupting their normality. To criticize is in this sense a practical and reflective way of exercising one's political freedom. The point of getting free of oneself – which pivots around the theme of limits and transgression and shows that objectivation and subjectivation are two sides of the same coin – is to engage in freedom that only exists by being exercised and tried out. 'Our real freedom is', says Rajchman (1985: 123), 'found in dissolving or changing the politics that embody our nature, and as such it is asocial or anarchical' and thus 'never finalizable, legislatable, or rooted in our nature'. This is yet another argument that Foucault's account of freedom as an ethical value cannot function as a standardized norm. The reason is that it does not attain the status of a universal since it is bound to what is situational and practical, and hence that freedom is antithetic to deductive schemes.

In discussing objectivation, emphasis is put on the becoming of objects, including that of the subject, which is a process ingrained in relations of power/knowledge. This is another way of saying that subject/object is not simply given either as an empirical fact or as a transcendental category. Instead, objects are made vis-à-vis the reduction of 'limit-experiences to objects of knowledge' (RM: 71). This is at the same time the making of the history of truth and the coming into being and circulation of truth games in which the subject becomes an object for knowledge. Foucault thus focuses on 'the processes of subjectivation and objectivation that make it possible for the subject qua subject to become an object of knowledge, as a subject' (F: 460). They unfold in a tense relationship with the enforcement of limits as to what can and what cannot be said and done. We are here dealing with a theme that occupied Foucault especially in his early and late works, which incorporates both ontological and critical aspects, and which, in addition, stresses the role of political authority. Note, for example, the early Foucault's comments on positivism that, 'if the medical character could circumscribe madness, it was not because he knew it but because he mastered it; and what positivism came to consider as objectivity was nothing but the converse, the effects of this domination' (HM: 505–6).

As mentioned earlier, the issue is not so much to discover scientific truth, as it is to go into the conditions of possibility of games of truth; and this involves an analysis of the becoming of the object and the settling of the rules of engagement. This is the archaeological dimension. It is in this field of the political authorities and their critics that the triangulation of power, knowledge and ethics becomes relevant. This is clear when Foucault (PPP: 386) briefly describes of what has been his goal: 'I have tried to see how the formation of psychiatry as a science, the limitation of its field, and the definition of its object implicated a political structure and a moral practice.' Critical engagement lies in the double move of exploring, on the one hand, the formation of objects in orders of discourse and, on the other, to experiment with the possibility of transgressing these limits and to play out games of truth and power with a minimum of domination (ESF: 298). So again, we see the experiential, reflexive and probing approach guided by the critical enlightenment ethos of downplaying the aspect of domination in power relations. This goes hand in hand with setting individuals free, politically speaking, that is, as opposed to chaining them to universal or communitarian normative standards invented by 'philosophical experts' as Rawls sarcastically labelled philosophers who would not act as citizens amongst others when taking part in political interaction.

Critical ontology of ourselves and political orientation

In Figure 4.1, I set out to combine two discussions, both of which are important for modern democratic politics. This is, on the one hand, Foucault's discussion of the critical ontology of ourselves and, on the other, his later analyses of liberalism where I will look at his distinction between revolutionary and radical approaches to government, which has not attracted much attention. The idea is to further the argument that Foucault's inside-out approach to politics goes along with a practical and experiential as opposed to a normative and ideological take on freedom.

Turning to Foucault's argument on the differences between revolutionary and radical approaches, the first thing to note is that it illustrates a difference between two types of critique and, more fundamentally, between two forms of political orientation.[12] On the one side, we have one that is lodged in the extra-political realm of law, which can be the natural law of social contract theory or universal laws of history as those found in Marxism. On the other side, we have critique based in the political realm of governmental practices, which is geared to the political authorities and their critics. Since the French revolution, the former is associated with emancipatory narratives of turning society upside-down 'so as to produce the overall programs of another society, of another way of thinking, another culture, another vision of the world', which Foucault occasionally refers to as global or radical projects.[13] According to this line

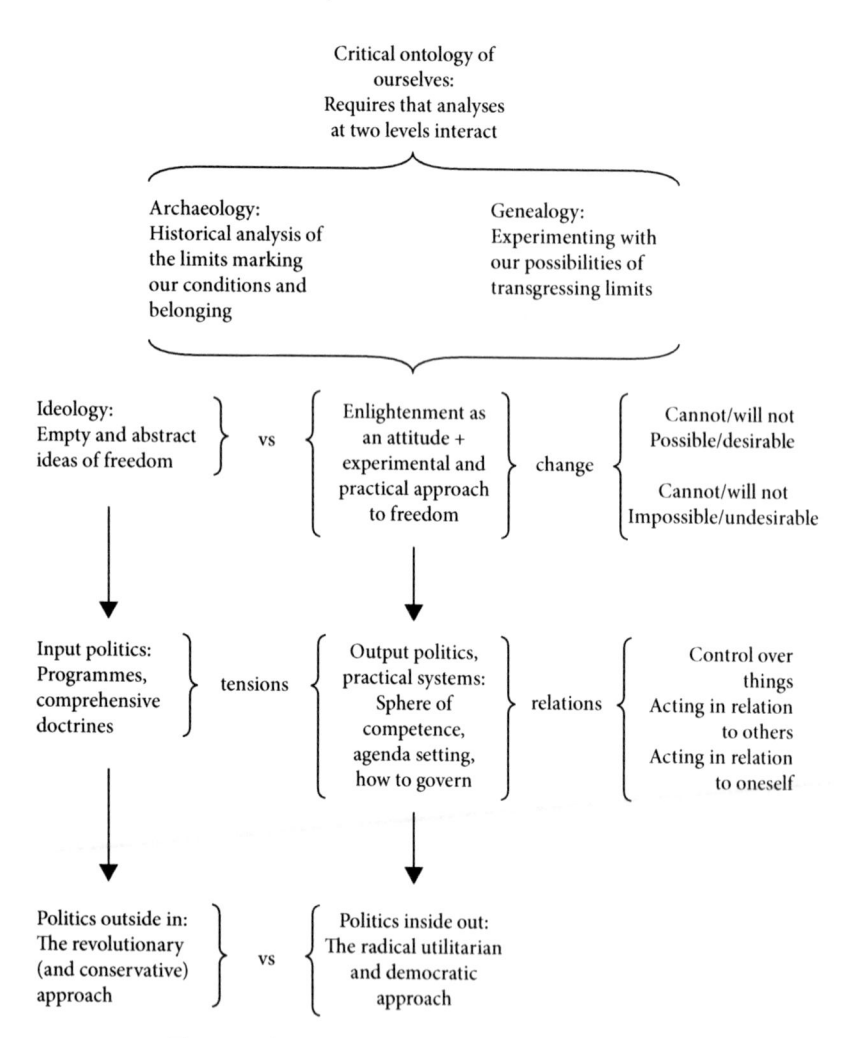

```
                    Critical ontology of
                         ourselves:
                    Requires that analyses
                    at two levels interact
        ┌─────────────────────┴─────────────────────┐
   Archaeology:                              Genealogy:
   Historical analysis of                    Experimenting with
   the limits marking                        our possibilities of
   our conditions and                        transgressing limits
   belonging
        └─────────────────────┬─────────────────────┘

Ideology:           ⎫        ⎧ Enlightenment as ⎫         ⎧ Cannot/will not
Empty and abstract  ⎬  vs    ⎨ an attitude +    ⎬         ⎪ Possible/desirable
ideas of freedom    ⎭        ⎪ experimental and ⎬ change  ⎨
                             ⎪ practical approach⎪        ⎪ Cannot/will not
    │                        ⎩ to freedom       ⎭         ⎩ Impossible/undesirable
    │                                │
    ▼                                ▼
Input politics:     ⎫        ⎧ Output politics,  ⎫        ⎧ Control over
Programmes,         ⎬tensions⎨ practical systems:⎬relations⎪ things
comprehensive       ⎪        ⎪ Sphere of         ⎪        ⎨ Acting in relation
doctrines           ⎭        ⎪ competence,       ⎪        ⎪ to others
                             ⎪ agenda setting,   ⎪        ⎪ Acting in relation
    │                        ⎩ how to govern     ⎭        ⎩ to oneself
    │                                │
    ▼                                ▼
Politics outside in:⎫        ⎧ Politics inside out:
The revolutionary   ⎬  vs    ⎨ The radical utilitarian
(and conservative)  ⎪        ⎪ and democratic
approach            ⎭        ⎩ approach
```

FIGURE 4.1 *The critical ontology of ourselves vis-à-vis revolutionary vs radical approaches to public political authorities*

of reasoning, which is anchored in the model of sovereignty, freedom goes together with attempting to neutralize or eliminate political power, the most far-reaching vision of which is the Marxist one of the withering away of the state under communism. The latter, by contrast, accentuates that the critical attitude links up with 'the great process of society's governmentalization' (WC: 48), which means that critique from the outset is grounded in political practice. This indicates that it is a pragmatic approach of negotiating the terms of exercising political authority, which primarily involves defining where to draw the line of the scope of government and the independence of the governed. Freedom lies here and makes sense only in relation to the political game of agonistic encounters.

The revolutionary approach, which is caught up in an ideological type of thinking and which is, moreover, epitomized by the French revolution, continued the tradition of opposing the power of government from the outside, that is, by the system of law. Public law is an external limitation on political power, and it is in this respect oppositional since 'the opposition always makes a legal objection to *raison d'État* and consequently uses juridical reflection, legal rules, and legal authority against it' (BB: 9). This way of arguing starts 'from the rights of man in order to arrive at the limitation of governmentality by way of the constitution of the sovereign' (BB: 39). The key issue is to ascertain 'the conditions under which the sovereign's rights can be exercised legitimately', which means that the 'problem becomes how to set juridical limits to the exercise of power by a public authority' (BB: 39; see also HS1: 86–90). As Foucault argues elsewhere (SMD: 26), the point is that 'the essential function of the technique and discourse of right is to dissolve the element of domination in power' and replace it with 'the legitimate rights of the sovereign ... and the legal obligation to obey'. The argument thus takes off from the natural rights of individuals and moves on 'to define under what conditions, for what reason, and according to what ideal or historical procedures a limitation or exchange of rights was accepted' (BB: 39). Such a limitation, which was in line with the social contract tradition of the eighteenth century, depended upon a differentiation between the rights agreed to be imprescriptible, as they ultimately stemmed from God, and those the citizen body could agree to cede. This would carve out a space for the legitimate power of sovereignty and the judicially defined liberty of citizens. It was at the same time a space in which disciplinary power could flourish invisibly, as it were, because it operated with another logic than legal power with its restrictive and visible limitations on liberty (BB: 10). It should thus be clear that the revolutionary approach is formed within a juridico-discursive representation of power: it is based on the model of sovereignty, it orbits around the question of legitimacy, it operates with the repressive hypothesis of power and it provides a juridical definition of liberty and, one could add, a normative foundation for critique.

The other approach, the radical one, is distinctly modern. It is advanced by English utilitarian thinkers and closely associated with the rise of the political economy. For them the problem was not the abuse of sovereignty and questions of legitimacy/illegitimacy but instead excessive government and success/failure (BB: 13–16). The idea is to avoid the externality between law and government we find in the legal model of power, where the risk is that law paralyses the possibility of governing, whilst it is acknowledged that it is necessary to limit the power of government. Limits are factual instead of being abstract and ideological, and they are internal and not external to government, which means that they are political instead of juridical and ultimately theological (BB: 10–11). Henceforth, the crucial difference compared to the revolutionary approach is that these limits, and, consequently, the parameters of critique and freedom, are defined vis-à-vis governmental practices as opposed to be given beforehand and formulated in an abstract philosophical and judicious language. This implies that they must be seen as desirable, that is, 'as the good limits to be established precisely in terms of the objectives of governmentality', which relates to resources, population, the economy and so forth – in a word, security (BB: 27). The juridical limitations on public political authorities are, in other words, defined in terms of governmental utility (BB: 43).

What we have here is an inside-out view of politics in which the revolutionary critique conducted in terms of the 'necessary limitation' of government – which is ultimately an expression of political theology – has been converted into an internal political and 'practical critique that takes the form of a possible transgression'. This move is thoroughly political as it finds its limits within the field of governmentalization and its values are immanent in this field. In addition, Utilitarianism is far from being an ideology that frames political authorities as legitimate domination from the outside. It is more likely a governmental technology, which is radical since it continually reflects upon the usefulness of governmental intervention and regulation, and calls for perpetual change. It does this by attempting 'to define the sphere of competence of government in terms of utility on the basis of an internal elaboration of governmental practice' focusing on what is and what is not on the agenda, or what ought to be on the agenda and what should be taken off the agenda (BB: 41, see also 12).

With his argument against conformism and abstract ideology Foucault places himself squarely in-between conservative and revolutionary

TABLE 4.2 *Two ways of constituting the regulation of public authorities by law*

	Revolutionary	Radical
Approach	The axiomatic juridico-deductive approach	The inductive and residual approach (governmental practice)
Starting point	Natural/original rights given prior to political authority	Governmental practice and its necessary limitation, both de facto and ideal
Structured around	Traditional positi\on of public law fixing the legitimacy of sovereignty and the duties of citizens to obey	The economy of government reason, defining the sphere of governmental competence in terms of the utility of intervention
Conception of law	System of will-law, expression of collective will: rights as those individuals have accepted to cede and those they will hold on to	The law as effect of transactions separating the sphere of intervention of public authorities from individual independence
Conception of freedom	Juridical conception based in rights of man: natural, original or basic rights that are inalienable	Political freedom as the independence of the governed with regard to government

approaches to moral codes. That is, he does not accept that individuals must either abide to the code of moral conduct or to its mirror image, the revolutionary maxim, or the Jacobin imaginary, of being outside and destroying it. In his radical alternative, where critique is not a demolition job, individuals are called upon to engage in the freedom of thought to reflect on the codes/norms and by experimenting and being curious, and thereby changing them. The differences between revolutionary and radical ways of approaching how public political authorities ought to be regulated by law is shown in Table 4.2, which paraphrases Foucault's argument.

Notes

1 See Lakoff 2008: 5–11 where he criticizes 'old Enlightenment reason' for relying on an illusory rationalism concerning utility, self-interest, knowledge and so on.
2 GE: 262; see also Bernstein 1991: 154, 163–5; Farrell 1989: 40; Rajchman 1985: 37–8.
3 WC: 47; WE: 100; GSO: 133–4; Miller 1994: 301–3. Foucault takes up all of these aspects of critique and taking care of oneself in his discussions of *parrhesia*.

4   PST: 137. Together with Glucksmann, Lévy and others, says Paras (2006: 89), 'the pivotal event of the twentieth century was not an epistemological one but a political one: not the death of man but the birth of the Gulag.'
5   ESF: 295–6; see also Nikolinakos 1990: 129, 131 and Jenkins 2011: 170. Owen (2002: 227) contrasts the ideal of rational dialogue envisaged in Critical Theory with Foucault's Nietzschean perspectivist approach to dialogue. The latter is geared to autonomy seen not only as self-reflection and choice but also in practical terms as the ways in which we conduct or govern ourselves and others. See Owen 1999: 36.
6   Foucault clarifies Kant's use of 'public' in the first lecture he delivered in 1983: 'The public is a reality established and delineated by the existence of institutions like learned societies, academies, and journals, and what circulates within this framework.' GSO: 8.
7   As to Foucault's non-judgemental approach to critique, see MP: 326. There might be a number of reasons for Foucault's scepticism towards this kind of projects. I have dealt with his criticism of the generalizations and abstract statements of Ideology Critique, which tend to explain everything and nothing. Other reasons have to do with his libertarian hostility to totalitarian political systems and his concern with the freedom of the individual. Finally, the French political and intellectual scene in the mid/late 1970s marked by the new philosophers' criticism of Marxism as paving the way for the atrocities of communist regimes could not avoid making an impact on Foucault, and it might have pushed him in a liberal direction. See, for example, Dews 1986: 61–77; Miller 1994: 238–40, 295–7; Paras 2006: 80–92.
8   Enlightenment is a way out. It is, says Kant (1997: 29), 'man's release from his self-incurred tutelage', which is self-incurred 'when its cause lies not in lack of reason but in lack of resolution and courage to use it without direction from another.' Enlightenment is thus an exit option, so to speak, which marks the difference between an authoritarian past and a possible future of self-government. WE: 99.
9   WE: 116. In his comments on Arendt he mentions that 'the network constituted by the power relations hardly allows for a decisive distinction' between power and domination. However, as Foucault says in WC: 66, 'one does not have to work with power understood as domination, as mastery.' The difference is between attempting to dominate and actual domination. Power should be thought about 'in such a way as to see how it is associated with a domain of possibility and consequently, reversibility, of possible reversal'. This leaves open whether power relations are, by definition, strategies of domination or can be conceived differently, for instance, as facilitating and empowering.
10 IT: 456. These two aspects are related to what Foucault in discussing discipline described as objectivation and subjectivation, respectively,

which are vehicles of how the modern subject is brought about. DP: 200–9; Rajchman 1984: 84–5.
11 HS2: 8. Here, he clarifies what has motivated him. See also his comments on 'the idea of a "limit-experience" that tears the subject from itself', which 'is really the theme that fascinates me.' RM: 31–2, 99. This is the issue of desubjectivation and the point where critical distance might become dangerous. For to be frank and to state what one believes is to expose oneself to risk that calls for personal integrity and courage. It is in this light one should see Foucault's appeal to the heroic.
12 I will only deal narrowly with the issue of revolutionary/radical. This means I will not go into Foucault's more elaborated discussions of revolution and how he changed his political outlook around 1976/1977 from being a revolutionary to becoming an outspoken critic of revolution and approaching a political liberalism of sorts. What matters here is the internal intellectual distinction between the two notions. For his discussion of revolution in relation to Kant's 'What is Enlightenment?' see GSO: lecture 1.
13 WE: 114. Foucault is not consistent in his use of the term 'radical'. Here he is using the term similarly to his use of 'revolutionary' in the bio-politics lectures.

5
The Nature of *Parrhesia*: Political Truth-Telling in Relation to Power, Knowledge and Ethics

Abstract: Parrhesia *is interesting for Foucault because it focuses on the political ground for exercising political authority, which is specific for democracy. It connotes truthful and trustworthy speech, which is entwined with the accountability and capability of democratic government. With* parrhesia *we get a political take on truth, for which personal integrity, frankness, timing, courage and resolve are defining features. The political ethos of parrhesia is readiness to challenge norms and rules, popular opinion and political authorities. Foucault's discussions of parrhesia are vital for getting at his political triangulation of power, knowledge and ethics, alias techniques of governmentality, truth-telling and the shaping of the relationship to self. This is the basis for approaching his discussions of the autonomy of politics and democratic political authority.*

Keywords: authorities/laypeople; democracy; power/knowledge/ethics; trustworthy; truthful

Dyrberg, Torben Bech. *Foucault on the Politics of Parrhesia*. Basingstoke: Palgrave Macmillan, 2014. DOI: 10.1057/9781137368355.0007.

Introducing Foucault's discussions of *parrhesia*

Parrhesia refers, as I have already mentioned, to the politically engaged person who as an authority or as a critic of authorities is trustworthy and speaks truthfully. It is a person for whom the issue at hand is what counts and who is, accordingly, ready to meet a challenge or an imminent danger head-on thus setting aside particularistic considerations, which are not relevant. *Parrhesia* is associated with Foucault's take on the enlightenment ethos of critique, which I dealt with in the previous chapter, just as it links up with his political resentment against domination and obedience. To speak up against popular opinion or powerful interests is risky, which takes personal integrity, good judgement and courage. In addition, it requires a sense of timing and – but this is more tricky – persuasive powers of rhetoric. What we have here is a distinctively political ethics, because it addresses the political relation *par excellence*, the authority/citizen axis, and takes into account the possibilities and risks pertaining to politics.

The political value of this conception of truth-telling lies in its close link to trustworthiness, which is connected with accountability. Both are of critical importance for democracy as they deal with how individual and collective agents enact and live their principles. In this respect it is related to acceptance/non-acceptance of authority, which is likewise a matter of doing. Moreover, it links up with accountability, reasonability and moral standing, but the point of stating trustworthiness and authority is to assert the practical *and* discursive nature of *parrhesia*. This should indicate that just as in critique we are not dealing with an epistemological take on truth as we find it in modern philosophy from Descartes onwards, where truth is an inner conviction of certainty concerning the nature of the external world (GSO: 68, 349–50; FS: 14; HS: 15–19; Stone 2011: 143–6). *Parrhesia*, by contrast, is a political concept, which is intertwined with the attitudes and decisions of individuals based on an assessment of their trustworthiness as well as their boldness and courage when it comes to deciding and acting. It is right from the start related to government in general and democratic government in particular. And governing is, says Foucault (HS: 404), 'a stochastic art, an art of conjecture, like medicine and also navigation: Steering a ship, treating a sick person, governing men, and governing oneself all fall under the same typology of rational and uncertain activity.' *Parrhesia* is the late Foucault's key to unlock several vital problem areas of politics.

This is, for instance, clear when he says, 'we see the problem of politics (of its rationality, of its relationship to the truth, and of the character who plays it) emerge around this question of *parresia*' (GSO: 159). This question cannot be categorized as either descriptive or prescriptive as it is essentially bound up with the political practice of being able to govern, passing judgements, critiquing, acting and so forth.

Parrhesia is geared to a commitment on the part of the individual citizen to address common concerns when the political community faces particular challenges or threats, which call for action. What is at stake in *parrhesia*, says Foucault (HS: 372, emphasis added), is 'the frankness, freedom, and openness that leads one to say *what* one has to say, *as* one wishes to say it, *when* one wishes to say it, and in the *form* one thinks is necessary for saying it'. If this were an epistemological statement of truth, it would hardly make sense and we would in any case be in 'the everything goes' genre, and the same would hold when seen from the angle of normative social and political theory. It is a political approach to truth, for which frankness, timing, courage, personal integrity and, indeed, the forming of the self as a citizen, a political being are defining features (GSO: 66–8). In short, we are dealing with individual capabilities, powers, which are fostered in a political community. *Parrhesia* is not then rule-bound activity, but an ability that is cultivated and trained over time and enacted in situations. It links up with perspectivism and value pluralism, since it does not exclude differences but proliferates them in agonistic encounters with unpredictable outcomes. Hence, *parrhesia* is inseparable from political power, and it is antithetic to epistemological and normative accounts of truth and the good life/society.

Parrhesia is interesting for Foucault because it focuses on the political ground for exercising political authority – one that defines the field, condition or logic, which is specific for democracy. The setting of *parrhesia* is the political scene, which is either that of the public democratic assembly involving the citizenry at large or the political authorities where *parrhesia* functions in relation to counselling, that is, the philosopher advising the political ruler. These are the two forms of *parrhesia* that Foucault takes up. The political ethos of *parrhesia* is a limited experience of sorts as it challenges conventions, norms and rules, popular opinion and political authorities. The key words of *parrhesia* are truth, reason and courage, which suggest that the term is related to power and critique. 'We should look for *parresia* in the effect that its specific truth-telling may have on the speaker, in the possible backlash on the speaker from the effect it has on the interlocutor' (GSO: 56). Foucault's discussions of *parrhesia* are important for getting at the political triangulation of power, knowledge and ethics, which is clear when he speaks of *parrhesia* as being located in-between 'the obligation to speak the truth, procedures and techniques of governmentality, and the constitution of the relationship to self' (GSO: 45; see also Stone 2011: 146). The location of *parrhesia* in the triangle of knowledge, power and ethics is, moreover, the basis for getting at his grasp of the autonomy of politics and democratic political authority.

Parrhesia as political analytics, practice and ethos

Foucault discussed various aspects of *parrhesia* in his lectures in the last three years of his life, all of which are now published in English. They consist of his lectures at Berkeley in *Fearless Speech* and his lectures at the College de France in *The Hermeneutics of the Subject*, *The Government of Self and Others* and *The Courage of Truth*. In these lectures we are presented with a rich insight into several political facets of this concept, which were articulated in the city-state in Greek antiquity over a period of several hundred years. It does not seem too far-fetched to assume that, for Foucault, *parrhesia* is a key to unravel some of the fundamental dilemmas and challenges facing democracy. How come then that there are so few who have studied Foucault's lectures on *parrhesia* despite the fact that they are highly politically charged and that they are now accessible and several of them have been for some years now?

There might be several reasons for this neglect of concern for *parrhesia*; among them is that the typical image of Foucault's take on truth is of a cynic and a relativist, which fitted the fashionable postmodern trends from the late 1970s up to the early 1990s. Claims to truth as well as the voicing of political values, such as freedom, were likely to be seen as façades behind which the cunning forms of power as productive submission reigned by forming the subject as normalized and obedient. This is the predominant power/resistance approach characteristic of the genre of Critical Theory and the counterculture, which has informed much of the reception of Foucault's works. The possibility that Foucault could have something else on offer in his analyses of truthfulness and trustworthiness as well as how they are related to power and the subject, and that this is politically relevant and even pertinent from a democratic

DOI: 10.1057/9781137368355.0007

perspective, seems hardly to occur and, in any case it appears, difficult to digest.

For this reason, amongst other things, Foucault's discussions of *parrhesia* have not attracted much attention in a political context, and there is not, then, an appreciation let alone an understanding of what this concept means for Foucault's approach to power relations in general and political power in particular. It is then relevant to ask about the status of *parrhesia* in Foucault's work: is it a moral injunction that fits uneasily with his dislike of interpretation and his resentment against normative theory prescribing the good life or the good society, or is it a way to legitimize what ruling elites demand in order to govern more efficiently?

The short answer to these questions is 'no'. The argument I will advance is that *parrhesia* is not an anomaly in Foucault's work. On the contrary, it is of critical importance for his sustained efforts over the years to expose and criticize the various forms of obedience, which go together with hierarchical structures and states of domination. Thus the concern with *parrhesia* taps into Foucault's experiential political inclination to widen and deepen what he referred to as the 'games of liberty' or 'liberty as a practice'. The focus is, as it always was for him, that of political authorities and their critics. As such *parrhesia* is located at the centre of Foucault's many histories, because it addresses the key axis of these stories, namely the relationship between authorities and laypeople in institutionalized settings such as medical or penal institutions or security apparatuses. Although not formally political, they do partake, according to Foucault, in making up the political infrastructure of society – what he calls the 'domain of politics' (THS: 189), which I will come back to in the last chapter. In general, I will hold that *parrhesia* is a key to unlock the nature of the relations between political authorities and the wider political community via regime structures. This is important for assessing the determination of political authorities in doing what has to be done as well as the democratic qualities of the relationship between authorities and citizens.

Seen in this light *parrhesia* designates a political analytics, practice and ethos, which falls between the modern description/prescription divide. It cannot, therefore, be boxed into either empirical or normative political theory, but is rather what Foucault calls 'problematization', that is, 'how and why certain things (behavior, phenomena, processes) became a problem' (FS: 171, see also 170–3). It is an intervention and a way of coping with real situations that cannot be inferred from them. *Parrhesia* is not then a performative act, but an act of creation that comprises aspects of knowledge, power and ethics, which, according to Foucault, lies at the root of the critical tradition of the West. As the origin of critique it signals the speaking truth to power, which historically has been bound up with all kinds of retaliations ranging from public ridicule to risking one's life. This is, of course, the reason truth-telling takes courage and resoluteness. But it also goes the other way around as *parrhesia* holds the door open for the possibility that political power may speak the truth of what has to be done. One cannot simply dismiss the possibility that political authorities might be both able and willing to dissociate from their own partial interests in order to tell people what needs to be done. It should be kept in mind though that the speaking of truth by political authorities and the free speech of citizens are closely connected as they make up different parts of a democratic political community – parts which might easily conflict with one another. Whereas the former is geared to make a government better to govern the population, the latter focuses on expanding practices of equal freedom, which is amongst other things a way to keep political authorities accountable.

Three points are noteworthy here. First, with the discussions of *parrhesia*, Foucault launches, albeit implicitly, a political ethics that is based on what it means to act politically. He looks at endogenous political relations as opposed to approaching politics from the outside. This is contrasted with the predominant approach in normative political theory, which consists in importing moral standards from the outside, as it were, which typically means that a universal moral theory is applied to politics. Second, *parrhesia* and democracy are two sides of the same coin, which indicates that authorities and laypeople are part of a political culture marked by liberty and equality as opposed to domination and hierarchy. This includes two aspects: the critics who speak truth to power to reveal, for instance, repression, manipulation and hypocrisy, and the political authorities who set out to making decisions on behalf of society and governing the population. Third, truth-telling in a democracy is based on the autonomy of politics, which relies on three types of exclusions organized around power, knowledge and ethics: (1) the exclusion of social stratification and the adoption instead of the principle that citizens are free and equal and that meritocracy must reign; (2) the exclusion of demonstrative truth and hence that politics is a technocratic game for experts, and the espousal of another dimension of truth-telling as boldness and integrity; and (3) the exclusion of religious dogmatism and veto power and the concomitant adoption of the principle of the primacy of the reasoning of human beings in concert.

Methodological considerations in studying *parrhesia*: the triangulation of power, knowledge and ethics

When Foucault's texts are devoted, in whole or in part, to method or methodology, he usually reflects on how he does research and what he has been doing over the years, which is of general interest for getting at what has been the key themes in his work.[1] Here it is important to point out how his lifelong concern with the question of the relationships between self, power and truth led him to discuss *parrhesia* – conceived as free and courageous truth-telling – and what it means for democracy. I will concentrate my discussion of *parrhesia* to the political realm in general and the relationship between regime and community in particular.

In Foucault's research on prisons as well as in his earlier works, 'the target of analysis wasn't "institutions", "theories" or "ideology", but practices – with the aim of grasping the conditions which make these acceptable at a given moment' (QM: 75; see also WC: 61–2). Two things are important here. First, practices – in this case practices of imprisonment – refer to 'places where what is said and what is done, rules imposed and reasons given, the planned and the taken for granted meet and interconnect' (QM: 75). In this context it would not make much sense to distinguish discourse and practice, because statements and actions are intertwined. So, we can say that we are dealing with discursive practices. The point is to analyse regimes of practices and, and this is the second point, their ability of being accepted, that is, treated as authoritative. The couplet of authority and acceptance is practical in the above sense of referring to the way things are run as opposed to being a matter of rational agreement, moral respect or beliefs in legitimacy. Instead, it refers to what is factual and practical, namely that Foucault's idea of analysing regimes of practices was 'to study this interplay between a "code" which rules ways of doing things (...) and a production of true discourses which serve to found, justify and provide reasons and principles for these ways of doing things'.[2] The focus is, in other words, on power and truth, which is essential for dealing with *parrhesia*.

The theme that occupied Foucault for more than two decades 'is to see how men govern (themselves and others) by the production of truth'. This does not refer to 'the production of true utterances, but [to] the establishment of domains in which the practice of true and false can be made at once ordered and pertinent'.[3] Foucault's take on truth – that is, more precisely, the relation between the subject and truth as mediated by power – is 'to resituate the production of true and false at the heart of historical analysis and political critique' (QM: 79).[4] His way of dealing with the true/false distinction is to situate it in a political domain, which frames it, and it is, consequently, to see truth as practical as opposed to epistemological, critical as opposed to analytical and as something which is enacted as opposed to something that is demonstrated. This way of dealing with truth runs as a red thread through Foucault's work. It is the reason he stresses that the various aspects of truth are not restricted to propositions and statements, but are applicable 'to ways of being, ways of doing things, ways of conducting oneself, or forms of action' (CT: 220). It is, moreover, inseparable from the fact that Foucault always centred his attention on acting, conducting, governing, and like terms associated with discursive practices, all of which testify to his preoccupation with the output side of politics, which again links up with authority/acceptance. His emphasis on truth in politics as speaking freely in the political community, which includes both critiquing authorities and authorities telling people what has to be done, addresses this essential political relationship of authorities and laypeople as well as their corollary of governing and acceptance.

The authority/laypeople type of relationship might profitably be seen as the key axis of the numerous discussions Foucault takes up in different contexts. In his dealings with *parrhesia* in the Athenian city-state in antiquity it is the political authorities (rulers) in relation to the citizens; when he deals with madness in the asylums in early modernity it is the medical authorities (doctors) in relation to the patients; in discussing power as normalization in prisons it is the administrative personnel (the modern governing state) in relation to prisoners and with regard to sexuality it is the conglomerate of various professions (e.g. doctors and educators) in relation to children and deviants. These are variations of the authority/laypeople axis rotating around the ability to govern and to gain acceptance. These are discursive practices and experiences analysed vis-à-vis the triangulation of power, knowledge and self. This is a way of contouring the skeleton of Foucault's approach for around a quarter of a century (from madness to *parrhesia*), which, obviously, displays much variation and where different histories, discussions, points of view and the like might not always make up a consistent whole. This also goes for his lectures on *parrhesia* in which he 'produces a myriad of analytical distinctions and subdivisions that are neither schematized nor explicitly joined together' (Kromann and Andersen 2011: 226).

However, my concern is neither to be the judge of possible inconsistencies and fallacies, nor to join Foucault's rich and somewhat unsystematic treatment of *parrhesia*. Two things matter. First, Foucault explores *parrhesia* from within the same parameters of the triangle (power/knowledge/self), but in contrast to his disciplinary period of normalizing power, he focuses on citizens and their relationship with political authorities in order to outline the specificity of the public political terrain. Second, on this basis he shows the entwined nature of *parrhesia* and democracy as well as their challenging relationship. The primary issue is how the democratic ethos of liberty and equality is related to ascendance, and hence how the power of democratic political authority can avoid being hierarchical and thrive on domination/obedience. I am, in other words, interested in the political aspects of *parrhesia* as opposed to those related to, for instance, pedagogical discourses of education.

To pursue this focus, Foucault had to clarify that to govern oneself and others via the production of truth entails that truth cannot be antithetic to power as such, but only to those forms of power that cripple our capacities to act (TP: 131, 133). This implies that political power can be seen in line with the etymology of the word as the ability to do something as opposed to being seen as essentially revolving around domination, which is motivated by the purpose of thwarting others' desires or interests. As mentioned in the first chapter, although the relationship between power and domination is somewhat slippery in Foucault's work, he does argue against reductionist accounts of power in terms of discipline amongst other things. More importantly, his overall objective during two decades only makes sense in light of the 'power to' angle of being able to work out particular results, which does not, as already mentioned, allude to a lenient and consensus seeking type of power. This is clear when he states that 'power is less a confrontation between two adversaries or their mutual engagement than a question of "government"', and to govern and to manage possibilities, he goes on, is 'to structure the possible field of action of others' (SP: 341). This is what is primary about political power relations, which means that it is secondary whether governing others implies domination; or rather it is a question of what actually happens when power is exercised. Truth is a way to structure action, that is to say, the production of truth is a means to govern self and others. It is this discursive practise of truth Foucault (FS: 5/169–70) looks at when he holds that his 'intention was not to deal with the problem of truth, but with the problem of the truth-teller, or of truth-telling as an activity: who is able to tell the truth, about what, with what consequences, and with what relations to power...'. This activity is caught up in the power/knowledge/ethics triangle framing political engagement, which is, as we saw in the previous chapter, important for discussing critique. In a democracy, *parrhesia* builds on the freedom of speech, which goes hand in hand with an egalitarian political set-up, each citizen counting as one. But there is more to *parrhesia* than the mere license to speak, to say whatever one wants to say, which has to do with the frankness with which one speaks and the 'obligation to tell the truth on the one hand, and an obligation accompanied by the danger that telling the truth involves on the other' (GSO: 300; see also 56, 315–16). It is this way of speaking and the obligation to do so, which the individual takes upon him or herself that interests Foucault, and which, moreover, lies at the heart of the problematic issue of equality/inequality in democracy, which I will return to shortly.

Although Foucault took up *parrhesia* only in the last couple of years of his life, his approach to the relationship between truth and the subject vis-à-vis power – that is 'from the point of view of the practice of what could be called the government of oneself and others' (CT: 8) – marks a continuity of his work. This is, for instance, clear when he inserts the self in the political terrain by holding that the problem he has dealt with 'has always been the question of truth, of telling the truth, the *Wahr-sagen* – what it is to tell the truth – and the relation between telling the truth and forms of reflexivity, of self upon self' (SPS: 446). In his discussions of *parrhesia* Foucault continues not only this theme of *Wahr-sagen*, but also the methodological set-up of triangulation (CT: 8; GSO: 42). It is this relation between truth-telling and mode of life in a public political context Foucault spelled out and probed in the last part of his life, and which is seen in the context of three interconnected types of practices: modes of veridiction, processes of governing and technologies of the self, alias knowledge, power and subject, whose joint articulation he terms 'focal points or matrices of experience like madness, criminality, and sexuality' (GSO: 41, see also 3, 45). The flip side of practice is experience, a term Foucault uses from madness to *parrhesia*. Experience, does not rely on individuals' emotional or cognitive state of mind, just as it is not a matter of contrasting 'a perceiving subject and a world of objects' (O'Leary 2010: 180). On the contrary, the subject 'continued to be understood as an entity wholly constructed in practices' (Paras 2006: 122), which in turn is situated in the intersection between the three axes of Foucault's enquiry. Thus in the introduction to *The Use of Pleasure* (HS2: 4) Foucault mentions that he set out to write 'a history of the experience of sexuality, where experience is understood as the correlation between fields of knowledge, types of normativity, and forms of subjectivity in a particular culture'. Experience thus takes form in the interplay between 'the three axes of any system of human activity, namely the relation to things (knowledge), the relation to others (power), and the relation to self (ethics)'.[5]

There are a couple of closely linked points that should be mentioned about the analysis of particular experiences according to the correlation of the three axes or elements constituting them (GSO: 41). They concern practice vs object, a theoretical shift and relationalism vs reductionism. These axes are themselves made up by discursive practices, which is to say that bodies of knowledge, norms of behaviour governing people and the constitution of the self are historical constructs, which have gone through processes of sedimentation and have turned out to be regulated forms of veridiction, that is, ways of producing the truth. The emphasis on process implies that they are not fixed entities, since relations of power/knowledge are immanent in these practises and these relations 'are not static forms of distribution, they are "matrices of transformations"'.[6] The focus on practice is accentuated by what Foucault terms 'a triple theoretical shift'. It involves, first, a shift from the theme of acquired knowledge to that of specific modes of veridiction; second, a shift from the theme of power as domination to procedures of governing people's conduct, which is the issue of governmentality, and third, a shift from the theme of the theory of the subject to the pragmatics of the subject and techniques of the self (CT: 9; GSO: 4–5, 41–2). Finally, it is important for Foucault to state that the complex relations between the three distinct elements, which together constitute specific experiences, are irreducible, meaning that one cannot be reduced to the other, as each of them plays a role in constituting experience. It follows that the discursive practice of sexuality, for example, 'must not be analysed simply as the surface of projection of [...] power mechanisms', just as 'to reduce knowledge [...]

to power, to make it the mask of power in structures, where there is no place for a subject, is purely and simply a caricature'.[7]

Why is *parrhesia* interesting for Foucault?

Why it is important to discuss *parrhesia* and what is in it for Foucault, and how is it fruitful for grasping political governing in general and democratic politics in particular? It is important to note that *parrhesia* is not an ethical encounter of how individuals ought to behave in relation to themselves and one another or how citizens should manage themselves in public forums. *Parrhesia* is not a normative theory in which among other things moral, cognitive and anthropological assumptions are worked into comprehensive doctrines of what individuals need to lead a good life and what constitutes a good society, as in, for example, Habermas and Honneth. *Parrhesia* is not a comprehensive doctrine, but it is worked out for the political realm in general and for democratic politics in particular. It is a key to unlock essential features of the interplay between power, knowledge and ethics organized around the axis of authorities and laypeople, whose reality principle or guideline is political practice and experience.

Parrhesia is interesting for Foucault for a number of reasons. First, it makes it possible for him to find a *political* ground as opposed to one that is immersed in sociology or philosophical anthropology, which will make it possible to evaluate democratic political authorities and political rationalities, broadly speaking. *Parrhesia* is of critical importance for getting at the power/knowledge/ethics triangle that occupied Foucault, and it is especially relevant in relation to normative theory, which typically claims that a firm normative foundation is mandatory for engaging in critique. This is, as we saw, the position of Critical Theory à la Habermas, Fraser and others, which is unacceptable for Foucault who is not normative in this way. *Parrhesia* is a form of critique as is modern philosophy if we, as Foucault suggests (GSO: 353–4; see also FS: 17–18), 'read it as a history of veridiction in its parrhesiastic form'. And, he goes on,

> It is a practice which rests its reality in its relationship to politics. It is a practice which finds its function of truth in the criticism of illusion, deception, trickery, and flattery. And finally it is a practice which finds the exercise of its practice in the transformation of the subject by himself and of the subject by the other.

His specific interest in the notion of *parrhesia* circles around the difference between, on the one hand, the constitutional right of every citizen to speak freely (*isegoria*) and 'the courageous and singular speech which introduces the difference of a truth-telling into the debate, on the other. It is this tension between a constitutional equality and an inequality stemming from the actual exercise of democratic power that interests Foucault' (Gros in GSO: 381–2). Thus *parrhesia* and democracy are inextricably linked, yet this relationship is also marked by tensions as inequality grows out of the ethos of equality amongst other reasons because this ethos advocates the principle of meritocracy.

Two issues are especially relevant, both of which touch upon the nature of critique – or better, they frame critique. First, *parrhesia* is a way to mark the specificity of political reasoning and the autonomy of politics, and second, it is a way to single out what specifically characterizes the power of political authority in a democracy. 'With the question of the importance of telling the truth,' says Foucault (FS: 5/169–70), 'knowing who is able to tell the truth, and knowing why we should tell the truth, we have the roots of what we could call the "critical" tradition in the West.' He summarizes his approach to *parrhesia* when stating that it 'is a verbal activity in which a speaker expresses his personal relationship to truth, and risks his life because he recognizes truth-telling as a duty to improve or help other people (as well as himself)' (FS: 19). There are several personal qualities and challenges at stake here, which I will touch upon. The personal relationship to truth has nothing to do with a subjectivist or solipsistic everything goes attitude. On the contrary, it poses challenging demands on the individual. It requires sincerity, reasonability and education; to risk one's life takes dedication, courage and willpower; to conceive truth-telling as a duty calls for freedom and impeccable moral standing, and to care for oneself and others entails generosity and a strict focus on the issue at hand.

It is no surprise then that *parrhesia* points at the link between being free and telling the truth. There are three reasons to tell the truth, which should be seen in the context of the power/knowledge/ethics triangle. They orbit around an understanding of politics as distinct from other types of practices and experiences by focusing on the authorities/laypeople axis and, consequently, the political culture: (1) In relation to the political power of governing, being truthful aims at grasping power and exercising political authority in a way that benefits the political community by specifying the challenges and tasks it faces (*ergon*) and being able to grasp the opportune moment (*kairos*) to act. Generally speaking, this angle sheds light on what characterizes the specificity of political practice organized around the axis of authorities and laypeople, that is, to tell what has to be done and critiquing those in power. (2) In relation to knowledge or veridiction, the point concerning freedom of speech implies that to be open and frank is the best way to deal with problems to avoid confusion and misunderstandings. Without the freedom of expression, it is neither possible to exercise democratic authority nor to resist or criticize political power. This angle facilitates among other things an understanding of what is implied in the change of political intensity from input to output politics both at the level of political discourse and governing. (3) In relation to the public political ethics of governing self and others, to speak truthfully and to focus on the issues at hand and how to deal with common concerns is the only way to convince people who are free and equal, and who have confidence in themselves and are capable of acting in concert. This angle clarifies what it means to speak of a political ethics which is freestanding in relation to its environment; that is, one that is developed within the political domain in light of power relations, possibilities, situations and so forth.

Parrhesia as a key to understanding democratic politics

When *parrhesia* is located in the triangle of knowledge, power and ethics, when it zooms in on the authority/laypeople axis with regard to governing and critiquing and when it concerns how people govern themselves and others via the production of truth, then there is no place for the standard conceptual repertoire of mainstream and critical research, both of which are steeped in the dualisms of civil society vs the state, consensus vs coercion and legitimacy vs illegitimacy. Instead of outlining a normative framework for democratic politics, Foucault's interest is geared to the practical and essential issues of politics: how to deal with issues of common concerns, how to secure acceptance and how individuality and commonality might coexist in the political community. In other words, the political issue is how reflexivity, self-esteem and toleration can go together in living with others and acting together. In contrast to defining them in opposition to each other as in the debates between liberals and communitarians in the 1980s, Foucault addresses the issue as one that concerns the relationship between authorities and laypeople in the political community. He treats politics as an autonomous practice as opposed to seeing it in derivative terms as a trade-off between the narrow self-interests of utility maximizing individuals, on the one hand, and their shared commitment to following the norms of what is morally good, on the other. Foucault sees in other words politics inside-out, as it were. In addition, he breaks new ground compared to how politics and democracy have usually been explored as the conversion of conflicting interests and identities into collective decisions. He looks at the output side of political processes more than the input side, which makes him focus more on how to act properly on concrete risks and possibilities than on how to aggregate preferences and integrate values into collectively binding decisions. In doing so he differentiates himself from both mainstream and leftist approaches, which are typically geared to the input side by examining how conflicting interests and identities acquire (or do not acquire) access to and recognition in political institutions.

Seen in this light *parrhesia* is the key to elucidate that a democratic order is antithetic to hierarchy and obedience, and their corollary, domination and manipulation. The reason is not only that democracy entails equality among citizens and the liberties that go with it, such as freedom of speech. The point is also that there can, as Foucault (HS: 382) says,

> only be truth in *parrhesia*. Where there is no truth, there can be no speaking freely. *Parrhesia* is the naked transmission... of truth itself. *Parrhesia* ensures... this transfer of true discourse from the person who already possesses it to the person who must receive it.

In this political reading, *parrhesia* is the medium of truth, which serves to facilitate the other's ability to take care of him or herself. *Parrhesia* is a means to ensure and facilitate the autonomy of oneself and others (HS: 379; see also WC: 49), and it is in this respect an opening, a possibility, an enactment of freedom that links up with power. In other words, it is a form of power that is not geared to secure the other's submission but to enhance his or her capabilities – an argument that could also be applied to collective entities in the political community.

As I said in the previous chapter, Foucault is taking issue with the perhaps most distinctive theme characterizing Western civilization, namely 'the paradox of the relations of capacity and [repressive] power', which has implied that 'the acquisition of capabilities and the struggle for freedom have constituted permanent elements' (WE: 115). The question is how the growth of capacities can be dissociated from the intensification of repressive power mechanisms. Foucault's interest in *parrhesia* – notably how it operates politically in a democracy – and hence the liberating power of speaking freely, reasonably and courageously, should be seen in this light. The various aspects of *parrhesia* attempt to answer this question by focusing on the intellectual and moral capabilities, which those who aspire to exercise the power of political authority need in order to govern well – capabilities designed and taught to supplement a democratic set-up as opposed to endangering the egalitarian and libertarian aspirations of democracy. Foucault intends in this way to raise the stakes of the enlightenment ethos of how the growth of capabilities can be disconnected from the intensification of repressive power and instead go hand in hand with the undefined and practical work of freedom.[8]

What does *parrhesia* have on offer for today's democratic politics?

There is a view that the late Foucault's discussions of *parrhesia* are both personal and political. This is not only due to the nature of *parrhesia* as the link between conviction, speech and deed, and hence the entering of a pact between the citizen and the political community of which she or he is part. It has also to do with the more general attitude characterizing Foucault's intellectual and political life, which *parrhesia* exemplifies, that he engages himself and allows himself to be carried away. This too is a pact in which one gives into curiosity, that is, the kind of curiosity 'which enables one to get free of oneself' (HS2: 8). Curiosity thus conceived is, Foucault goes on, a philosophical activity, 'an exercise of oneself in the activity of thought', one that endeavours 'to think differently, instead of legitimating what is already known' (HS2: 9). To get free, to think and perceive differently, to exercise and reflect and so on, all of this is antithetic to self-indulging complacency and goes instead hand in hand with engaging in intellectual as well as political risk-taking. This is what Foucault means by politicization, which I will come back to in the last chapter. Thus Foucault, says Bernstein (1991: 164), 'forces us to ask hard questions about our most cherished beliefs and comforting convictions'. It is this engagement and hence this way of exercising one's relationship to oneself – which pivots around honesty, courage and resolve – that marks the individual's entrance into the political realm, that is, its ability to conduct itself, to form a qualified opinion and informed judgement, in line with what Arendt (1968: 241–2) called an 'enlarged mentality' of reflective judgement in public life where we communicate with others by putting ourselves in the other's place as opposed to being absorbed by short-sighted and narrow-minded concerns (see also Foucault on moderation, HS2: 78–93).

Notes

1. QM; BB: lecture 1, 4, 8; GSO: lecture 1, 3; CT: lecture 1; HS: lecture 1; ST: 151ff. In addition, there are numerous extracts from interviews, lectures and articles where he reflects on how he works and what has always interested him.
2. QM: 79; see also 75 where he speaks of 'what is to be done', alias 'effects of "jurisdiction"' and 'what is to be known', alias 'effects of "veridiction"'.
3. QM: 79; see also SW: 8, where he mentions the problem he has dealt with in all his books: 'wie ist in den abendländischen Gesellschaften die Produktion von Diskursen, die (...) mit einem Wahrheitswert geladen sind, und die underschiedlichen Mactmechanismen und –institutionen gebunden?' Note also his earlier comments on truth in relation to ideology where he mentions that the problem is to see 'historically how effects of truth are produced within discourses which are neither true nor false'. Truth is understood as an 'ensemble of rules according to which the true and the false are separated and specific effects of power attached to the true', which is a battle of the status and role of truth; TP: 118, 132. It follows that this way of approaching the question of truth cannot be an epistemological one, but it is political. More specifically, it has to do with political authority.
4. Veyne (2010: 93) is onto something similar when mentioning that Foucault did not set out to outline 'a logical or philosophical theory of truth, but an empirical and almost sociological critique of telling the truth, that is to say the "rules" for speaking truly'. From my perspective it is more to the point to say that Foucault outlines a political critique.
5. Patton 2003: 519. See also WE: 117; PHS: 199–203 which is close to but not identical with the introduction to HS2; GSO: 3–5; CT: 8–9. For a discussion of Foucault's two conceptions of the term experience as 'everyday experience' and 'transformative experience', see O'Leary 2010.
6. HS1: 99. This is the second preliminary rule for studying discursive practices, which tie together power/knowledge: 'Rules of continual variations'. As Kelly (2013: 75) notes power/knowledge is about governing transformations as opposed to setting up static distributions or hierarchies.

7 HS1: 100 and CT: 8–9, respectively. The first quote is part of the fourth preliminary 'Rule of the tactical polyvalence of discourses'.
8 Cf. Foucault's linkage of *parrhesia* to Kant's *Aufklärung*, GSO: lecture 1. Moreover, there is a thematic link between Foucault and certain strands of Critical Theory with the exception, however, that the early Frankfurt School displayed an apocalyptic disillusionment with Reason's complicity with power. In speaking of the particular form of rationality characterizing the West, Foucault (IF: 273) asks, 'how can that rationality be separated from the mechanisms, procedures, techniques, and effects of power that accompany it and for which we express our distaste by describing them as the typical form of oppression of capitalist societies.'

6
The Politics of *Parrhesia*: The Autonomy of Democratic Politics and the Parrhesiastic Pact

Abstract: Parrhesia *is instrumental to sustain the autonomy of politics by bracketing religious dogma, social stratification and expert knowledge as the basis for decision-making by setting up a pact that binds the individual to his/her statement and the authorities to the community to assure their accountability and trustworthiness. The idea that underpins the autonomy of politics and democracy is that truth and a meritocratic principle of ascendency are two sides of the same coin. Democracy and* parrhesia *condition each other, but democracy might be undermined by the negative* parrhesia *of flattery and manipulation, which undermines democratic governing, as political power no longer unfolds in agonistic encounters. Hence, the tightrope balance between good and bad* parrhesia *illustrates the ambitious but fragile nature of democracy.*

Keywords: democracy; freedom/duty; generosity; good/bad *parrhesia*; parrhesiastic pact; secularization thesis

Dyrberg, Torben Bech. *Foucault on the Politics of* Parrhesia. Basingstoke: Palgrave Macmillan, 2014.
DOI: 10.1057/9781137368355.0008.

Democracy and *parrhesia*

Foucault discusses critique in relation to the enlightenment ethos of reason and liberty as well as in relation to different forms of liberalism, which delineate the principles and methods of modern government. In this chapter, I will deal with this focus on liberty as practice and political power as creative, together with the arguments concerning the autonomy of politics, which lies at the foundation of his discussion of *parrhesia* as free, true and courageous discourse. This discourse, moreover, links political authority and critique, which Foucault illustrates by what he terms as the circuit of *parrhesia*. The point here is to situate *parrhesia* in the context of political order, power struggles, truth and reasonability. Foucault's lectures on *parrhesia* are important for assessing the nature of political authority in a democracy as they clarify what specifically counts as the political principles of societal coexistence. Seen from this perspective, Foucault's *parrhesia* has affinities with Rawls's public reason as a scene of contestation and as rules of conduct and engagement in political dialogues and struggles in which contenders seek to persuade each other.[1]

With his discussions of *parrhesia* Foucault aims to pick out what might be seen as the single most significant contribution of Greek and Roman antiquity for European civilization, namely politics as an autonomous practice (HS3: 81–95). *Parrhesia* is crucial for bringing about a distinctively political logic, which is able to sustain the autonomy of political practice by excluding religious revelation and dogma, social stratification and expert knowledge as the basis for political discourse and decision-making. In doing so the autonomy of politics and democracy becomes two sides of the same coin, which paves the way for individuals being treated as free and equal and for pursuing a meritocratic principle of ascendance. This is important for setting up, accepting and assessing the quality of democratic authorities. The idea that underpins the autonomy of politics and hence democracy is that truthfulness and trustworthiness as well as ascendency ought to be seen as closely connected with one another.

Democracy and *parrhesia* condition each other, but democracy might also be undermined by the negative *parrhesia* of idle chat, which goes hand in hand with flattery and manipulation. The result is conformity, fear and censorship, which undermine democratic governing, as political power no longer unfolds in agonistic encounters. The tightrope balance between good and bad *parrhesia* is a reminder of the ambitious but fragile nature of democracy as a political construction. *Parrhesia* is not simply about convincing others, but primarily about setting up a covenant, which binds the individual to his/her statement and further to the political community. 'I am the person who has spoken this truth', says Foucault (GSO: 65), 'I therefore bind myself to the act of stating it and take on the risk of all its consequences.' This is a pact the individual enters with him/herself vis-à-vis the community in which there is a correspondence between reason and how one conducts oneself. The pact is a promise to match words and deeds, which in a political context means that there is a fit between the statements of political authorities and what they actually do. As Markovits argues (2008: ch. 5), the speaker's assurance of his/her sincerity is not enough as this might easily be a point where rhetoric takes over and *parrhesia* degenerates (Saxonhouse 2006: 92–3). This correspondence means that *parrhesia* sets out to bind the individual to him/herself and to the community, which is an assurance that political authorities are not out of joint with the political community, but are accountable and trustworthy.

Democracy and the parrhesiastic pact

A politically true discourse is one that is, first, based on and safeguards the autonomy of politics as opposed to one that is measured against a pre-political standard. The latter could, for instance, be a moral one of virtues as in communitarians or an epistemological, anthropological or eschatological construction of truth à la Habermas, Honneth and Marx, respectively. Second, it is one that convinces by way of public political reasoning and the practice of following it as opposed to ways of persuasion steeped in rhetoric and demagoguery. Foucault's political approach to power and truth implies that he does not see political power from the viewpoint of an equilibrium model where it is assigned the task of balancing instrumental and communicative logics. This is, amongst other places, clear in his negative attitude to the distinction between state and civil society, where politics is confined to the state and the function of politics is reduced to mitigate conflicting interests, on the one hand, and to strike a balance between the aggregation of preferences and the integration of norms in the civic culture.[2] By extension, truth is neither contemplative nor disinterested; that is, it is not concerned primarily with, say, assessing factual statements. Instead, it focuses on two things: with choosing political action, that is with making collectively binding decisions and implementing them *and* to secure the quality of political leadership and, therefore, how to exercise political power prudently and boldly. Finally, in both his discussions of security and critique/*parrhesia*, Foucault pays less attention to the input politics of identity and interests, and looks instead on the output politics of efficient government and how political authorities face challenges.

Just as Foucault stresses that *parrhesia* as fearless speech is articulated by people who are free and equal and that high status is neither necessary nor important (HS: 375; HS3: 85–6; GSO: 162), Rawls, is adamant to stress that politics is a matter for citizens as opposed to experts. 'In justice as fairness', he says in his debate with Habermas, 'there are no philosophical experts. Heaven forbid! But citizens must, after all, have some ideas of right and justice in their thought and some basis for their reasoning. And students of philosophy take part in formulating these ideas but always as citizens among others.'[3] *Parrhesia* is accessible to everybody and is guided by a meritocratic principle, which puts social status between brackets in public life, that is, when dealing with common concerns, and which, moreover, involves risk-taking and courage (GSO: 177–8; Markovits 2008: 68–9). These are among the reasons *parrhesia* is not a performative act if by that it is meant a statement, which is at the same time an act guided by certain rules in specific situations in 'a particular, more or less strictly institutionalized context' (GSO: 61), for instance a chairperson opening a meeting or a priest marrying a couple (GSO: 65). But in *parrhesia*, says Foucault (GSO: 62; see also FS: 13),

> whatever the usual, familiar, and quasi-institutionalized character of the situation in which it is effectuated, what makes it *parresia* is that the introduction, the irruption of the true discourse ... opens the situation and makes possible effects which are, precisely, not known. *Parresia* does not produce a codified effect; it opens up an unspecified risk.

There is, nonetheless, a common theme in Foucault and Habermas that revolves around that truth does something: it effects a change by convincing people – this is the function of truth (HS: 407). Whilst Habermas (1971: 154) draws attention to the paradox of the peculiar force of the better argument's absence of force – that in facing such an argument one must change one's opinion – the crucial theme in Foucault's *parrhesia* is to direct others through truth-telling (GSO: 158) by setting up a pact that connects individuals and authorities to the political community. It is not Habermas' paradoxical force/non-force or Lukes' rational persuasion, which is the equally peculiar result of bringing the opposites of free will and determination together, just as it is not brought about rhetorically although *parrhesia* might 'call upon methods of rhetoric. But it is not necessarily the objective and purpose of *parresia*' (GSO: 54; see also 53 and Lukes 2005: 36). *Parrhesia* is not, strictly speaking, persuasion although it can serve this function. Basically, it is the truth-telling by a trustworthy person, which might make use of rhetoric, but which might also be confrontational and antithetical to pedagogical approaches.

The type of persuasion we are dealing with in *parrhesia* concerns not only the truth of the statement but also that the one enouncing it truly believes it to be the truth. This focus on the truth-teller is, for instance, clear when Foucault contrasts *parrhesia* and rhetoric by saying that *parrhesia* 'is a discourse which does not owe its strength (its *dunamis*) to the fact that it persuades. It is a discourse which owes its *dunamis* to the fact that it springs from the very being which speaks through it' (GSO: 327). Here we have two levels and the point is to bind the individual 'to the content of the statement' and 'to the act of making it' (GSO: 65). The former concerns roughly speaking the reality of the statement: did the speaker get the facts right? Does he/she make sense? Is it a reliable interpretation of a particular situation, event, trend, challenge? Is it the best thing to do in this particular situation and so forth? The latter is 'the parrhesiastic pact', which is geared to ascertain the seriousness, trustworthiness and responsibility of the speaker as a citizen speaking on behalf of or as a critic of political authorities. In this personal commitment the person acting politically aims to convince the listener or the audience by stating: 'I tell the truth, and I truly think that it is true, and I truly think that I am telling the truth when I say it', and that 'I who am speaking am the person who judges these thoughts to be really true and I am also the person for whom they are true' (GSO: 64; HS: 404–5). Thus truthfulness requires respect for the two basic virtues of truth, which, in the words of Williams (2002: 11) is 'Accuracy and Sincerity: you do the best you can to acquire true beliefs, and what you say reveals what you believe.'

For a modern academic sentiment this is not much of an assurance and it might not have been either two-and-a-half millenniums ago. In any case, it is hard to imagine that a politician would get away with it, as this insistence on sincerity would be ridiculed as a cheap rhetorical trick. And most likely, it would be just that! However tempted one might be to indulge in such a sceptical attitude, one ought to keep in mind that the relative ease with which *parrhesia* might be corrupted is not an argument against its prominence in democratic politics. More importantly, one would have to look at the context of this claim; more specifically one would have to assess the trustworthiness of the person who thus spoke. Is it someone to be trusted, who gets the facts right, who has a good sense of judgement, who can act at the spur of the moment and who, generally speaking, has a good track record? If one were just looking for earnest and good intentions, one would be an easy victim of manipulative political communication.

In any case, the alternative of either eliminating morality in politics by equating might and right or to subsume might under right by appealing to pre-political communitarian bonds or abstract universal axioms is not an option for at least two reasons. First, these alternatives miss the point that what is at stake here is not a moral issue at all, but one that is concerned with the nature of the power of political authority and the integrity of the political realm. Second, they undermine the specificity and autonomy of politics by either turning it into a rubberstamp of what the most powerful demand or by depositing the integrity of political reason and practice among 'philosophical experts'. Seen in this light there is no alternative *within* the political scene to combine public political reason and *parrhesia* with their emphasis on liberty/equality and trust in the political community, that is, among citizens and between citizens and authorities.

Democracy and *parrhesia* condition each other, but democracy might also be undermined by negative *parrhesia*, which goes hand in hand with exercising repressive power by means of flattery and manipulation (GSO: 155, 168, 182–3). The latter signals the unavoidable and fragile difference introduced in the exercise of true discourses in a democracy. The tightrope balance between good and bad *parrhesia* should be seen as a reminder of the ambitious, but fragile, nature of the political construction of democracy, and hence of the autonomy of politics. *Parrhesia* is not simply about convincing others – here there is, of course, an affinity with rhetoric – but primarily about setting up a covenant of sorts. This pact goes beyond rhetoric and binds the individual to his or her statement and further to the political community, which we saw above. The parrhesiastic pact is, in the words of Miller (2006: 32), 'the act of free courage through which one links oneself to oneself in the act of truth-telling.'

Parrhesia is a correspondence between reason and how one conducts oneself (GSO: 56), which is to say that truth is disclosed in the event, which in turn is to say that 'the very event of the enunciation may affect the enunciator's being' (GSO: 68). The pact assures or promises a match between words and deeds, which in a political context means that there is a correspondence between the statements of political authorities and what they actually do. Says Foucault, 'the subject who speaks, and who speaks the truth, and the subject who conducts himself as this truth requires ... this [is a] perfect fit between the subject who speaks, or the subject of enunciation, and the subject of conduct' (HS: 406; see also FS: 97ff). Otherwise, it is not plausible to hold that the political authority has been guided by the truth, just as it is not possible to hold it accountable. As a political category *parrhesia* sets out to bind the individual, partly, to him/herself in order to underpin its personal integrity and moral standing, and partly, to the community to strengthen its political accountability and loyalty. To do that requires in both cases that words and deeds must not be out of joint as this would impair the trustworthiness of authorities and their critics as well as the accountability of democratic institutions (Markovits 2008: 50–60).

The parrhesiastic pact can, moreover, be seen in terms of generosity as it is dedicated to the issue at hand and meeting it head-on, that is, to solve a problem, meet a challenge, avoiding a catastrophe and so on. The political message – the authoritative communication – is not then covert just as it does not hide its real motives. To be able to communicate in this manner requires in addition a linking not only between discourse and practice, but also between discursive practice, on the one hand, and political task and timing, on the other. To live up to the parrhesiastic pact one must be prepared to perform a political task at the right moment, to reach out for that moment or to grasp it when it comes. This is the notion of *kairos*, 'the decisive or crucial moment or opportunity' (FS: 110), which is not only a question of timing but also of one's courage and care for oneself, which make it possible to act at the crucial moment. As Foucault says (HS: 406) when emphasizing the situational aspect of *parrhesia*: '*parrhesia* is free speech, released from the rules, freed from rhetorical procedures, in that it must ... adapt itself to the situation, to the occasion and to the particularities of the auditor.' Elsewhere he notes that 'what essentially defines the rules of *parrhesia* is the *kairos*, the occasion, this being precisely the situation of individuals with regard to each other and to the moment chosen for saying this truth' (HS: 384; see also FS: 111; GSO: 224, 227).

Politics as freestanding: political exclusion and *parrhesia*

The idea which underpins the autonomy of politics and democracy is that truth and ascendency ought to be two sides of the same coin. For this, Foucault outlines four qualities the politician must possess to 'be able to exercise through his *parresia* the ascendancy necessary for the democratic city to be governed – in spite of or through democracy' (GSO: 180). First, one has to be able to provide a truthful account of the problem at hand and to sort out what would be the appropriate thing to do, what is in the public interest. Second, this insight has only political value inasmuch as it is shared with others, meaning that one has to be able to communicate it. Third, one must be devoted to deal with the problem in the name of the public interest as opposed to use it as a foil for promoting one's own agenda. Fourth, one has to have a good track record, that is, be trustworthy by being 'morally reliable, honest, and incorruptible' (GSO: 180). The opposite situation marks the degeneration and corruption of democracy. This is the situation of bad *parrhesia*, of idle chatter and the prevalence of the worst desires. Here, 'the essence of the evil is the lack of the rightful ascendency of true discourse' (GSO: 201), which is the image of the tyrant whose way to, and stay in, power is not based on the difference made by a true discourse, but instead by flattery, manipulation, violence and so forth. This is poisonous for democratic governing and renders *parrhesia* virtually impossible.

In speaking of rightful ascendance, the idea is that those who aspire to political power should be fit for the job: they should be trustworthy, possess a sound sense of judgement and be courageous to be able to take bold action. In addition, they should be kept in a leash by the citizenry, which in contemporary societies imply the tripartition of powers and the setting up of rules that limit the risk of power becoming abusive. 'Against power one must always set inviolable laws and unrestricted rights', says Foucault (UR: 453). No guarantees can be provided against the abuse of power, but these are some of the means to minimize this risk. The most important one lies in the democratic set-up of agonistic power struggles

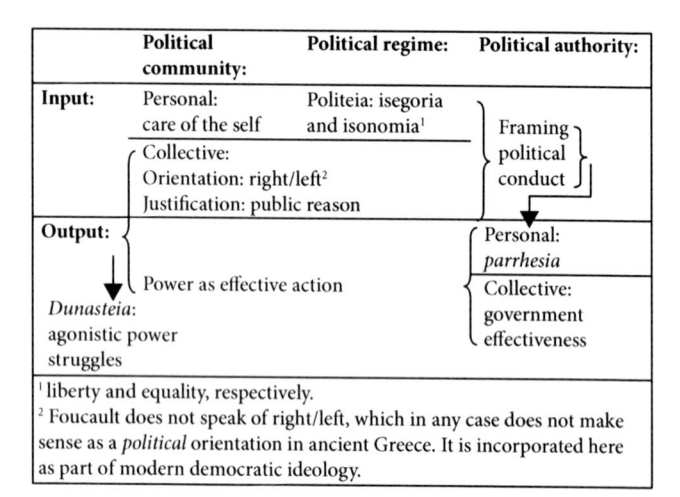

	Political community:	Political regime:	Political authority:
Input:	Personal: care of the self	Politeia: isegoria and isonomia[1]	Framing political conduct
	Collective: Orientation: right/left[2] Justification: public reason		
Output:		Power as effective action	Personal: parrhesia
	Dunasteia: agonistic power struggles		Collective: government effectiveness
[1] liberty and equality, respectively. [2] Foucault does not speak of right/left, which in any case does not make sense as a *political* orientation in ancient Greece. It is incorporated here as part of modern democratic ideology.			

FIGURE 6.1 *Input/output politics in relation to community, regime and authority*

and an informed and active citizenry both of which inhibit the monopolization of repressive power.

The significance of Foucault's arguments concerning the care of the self and *parrhesia* is that they manage to connect three axes of importance for grasping the specificity of politics, which complement or even illustrate his work on power, knowledge and ethics by giving them a political turn. The three axes are schematically illustrated in Figure 6.1. They consist of input and output politics, individual and collective action and the levels of political practice of community, regime and authority.

The condition of possibility for speaking about the autonomy of political practice and hence of the freestanding nature of public political reasoning lies in the secularization thesis: 'Athens is founded on the secularisation of parrhesia', says Szakolczai (2003: 180) and, he goes on, '[d]emocracy is positively based on parrhesia, negatively on the silence of the gods.' This secularization might have been the first of its kind and one that is as relevant as ever. Foucault speaks in a similar vein in his analysis of Euripides' play *Ion*. This is 'the decisive parrhesiastic play where we see human beings taking upon themselves the role of truth-tellers – a role which the gods are no longer able to assume' (FS: 27; see also GSO: 205). Later on he mentions that 'truth is no longer disclosed by the gods *to* human beings ... but is disclosed to human beings *by* human beings through Athenian *parrhesia*' (FS: 38), and elsewhere he stresses that the gods are not bearers of *parrhesia*, which is, on the contrary, 'a human practice, a human right, and a human risk' (GSO: 154). Interesting in this context is also Foucault's mentioning of the three differences between the authoritative speech of *parrhesia* and prophecy, that is, prophetic truth-telling:

- The parrhesiast speaks in his/her own name as a citizen and expresses his/her own opinion vs the prophet who speaks in the name of the deity.
- The parrhesiast unveils what is and exposes the interlocutor's blindness vs the prophet who foretells the future.
- The parrhesiast speaks as clearly as possible, the transparent truth vs. the prophet who speaks in riddles which calls for interpretation (CT: 15–16).[4]

Foucault had already broached the issue of secularization in the early 1970s, notably in his lectures in Rio in May 1973 when he spoke of the origin of Greek society in the fifth century BC, which inaugurated Western civilization – an origin that revolved around power/knowledge. In the archaic period truth had been a ritualized act inseparable from exercising power and a right assigned to certain privileged agents such as poets and oracles (Rayner 2010: 66). With the transition to the classical period, Greek society witnessed 'the dismantling of that great unity of a political power that was, at the same time, a knowledge – the dismantling of that unity of a magico-religious power' (TJF: 31). The union of power and knowledge disappeared, which gave way for a division of labour between politicians, experts and people, alias power, truth and memory. In the first place, 'political power is blind' and the political ruler, that is, 'the man of power would be the man of ignorance'. The philosopher, the seer, by contrast, is one who is 'in communication with the truth, the eternal truths of the gods or of the mind', and, finally, we have the people deprived of both power and knowledge, but 'who bore the memory or could still give evidence of the truth' (all the quotes, TJF: 32).

Foucault's research agenda in the early 1970s focused on dispelling the Western myth associated with Plato that '[w]here knowledge and science are found in their pure truth, there can no longer be any political power' (TJF: 32). This approach was, as he stated himself, inspired by Nietzsche, but it also had an affinity with Ideology Critique and later postmodern trends by seeking to reveal that behind knowledge and truth claims we find struggles for power and, therefore, contingency rather than objectivity. To understand critique in terms of revealing what is hidden, and what others attempt to cover over, remains largely the image of Foucault's genealogical critique: that which seems natural, given or unavoidable can be shown to have originated in power struggles; hence they are contingent and can change as opposed to being necessary and unchangeable (Hendricks 2012). However, with Foucault's lectures on *parrhesia* in the early 1980s we find a partly different reading of the dislocation between power and knowledge in the classical era. This one acknowledges the division of labour between rulers and philosophers, but does so by including the latter in the political field. What we get is a *political* take on truth that does not point back to an archaic 'magico-religious power'. Instead, it asserts the principles of modern democratic political community by providing a stronger underpinning of the secularization thesis, which is a major pillar of the autonomy of politics.

The idea is that human beings, or at any rate individuals acting politically, instead of being modelled in the image of their gods and seeking counselling and arbitration from them, are on their own, as it were, at least when doing politics. Human beings are, to put it differently, shaped in their own image, and it is this self-imaging that provides the political context for governing others vis-à-vis oneself. This is what turns the care of the self into an imperative for political education considered broadly as the building of political capital; and by the same token, this is also what grounds the imperative of effective governing in a democracy and calls for a meritocratic principle.

The secularization thesis plays a significant role in carving out a political discursive terrain, which has an intrinsic quality, since it cannot be inferred from or legitimized in terms of higher powers. These are religious as in the case discussed by Foucault, but although religion is a classical and exemplary case concerning toleration, it is, nonetheless, just one among numerous other types of comprehensive doctrines, which aim to ground the terms of political discourse. Other types could revolve around racist, sexist, culturalist or nationalist parameters. In any case, the innate quality of the political moment is founded negatively on the exclusion of what is antithetic to the freestanding nature of public political reasoning. Two types of exclusions are in play: the one already mentioned of religion, the other of social status. In addition, a third one could be mentioned, namely the truth claims of experts. This is what Foucault calls 'demonstrative truth', which is antithetic to *parrhesia*.

There are three types of exclusions in his argument dealing with the specificity and autonomy of politics, which underpin the equal liberty of citizens and prove decisive for getting at democratic politics and the appreciation of liberty as a practice. They revolve around social stratification (power), comprehensive doctrines (ethics) and demonstrative truth (knowledge). It is the last one I will look at now. But before doing that, I will mention briefly that the positive foundation takes off from the negation of these three exclusions, that is, the meritocratic principle irrespective of social status, the establishment of public political reasoning that is freestanding and *parrhesia*. In addition, knowledge focuses on those principles and techniques that underpin the input side of public political reasoning and the output side of effective government.

It is interesting to note that Foucault discussed truth-telling in a way that draws attention to his later discussions of *parrhesia* in a lecture in January 1974 (PP: 233–4) in which he made a distinction between two images of truth. The first one is conceived in relation to events amongst other things, which Foucault interchangeably referred to as 'truth-thunderbolt' and 'truth-lightening'. As in the case of *parrhesia*, truth is an event and the relationship between the truth-event and the person who is seized by it is 'a hunting kind of relationship, or, at any rate, a risky, reversible, warlike relationship' (PP: 237; see also 206, 210–1). The technology of this form of truth 'is linked to the event, to strategy, and to the hunt'; it is provoked by rituals, captured by ruses, seized according to occasions, and it is aroused and hunted down. This kind of truth as production belongs to the order of what happens, and it calls for strategy as it is based on power (PP: 239). Truth-thunderbolt is a technology of truth which, today, has been 'effectively dismissed, brushed aside and supplanted' (PP: 238) by the other image of truth, which has become the dominant one.

Whereas the first image of truth is more akin to the political realm and resembles *parrhesia*, the other, or second, image is that of 'truth-sky': the truth which is 'universally present behind the clouds' (PP: 237). Truth-sky belongs to the order of what is, and it is given in the form of discovery and through the mediation of instruments. It is something that is found and it is based on a 'technology of demonstrative truth joined ... to scientific practice' (PP: 236). In this epistemological image, the technology of truth calls for method as it is a matter of knowledge based on the subject/object relationship. Yet, as Foucault argued a few years earlier (WK: 212), '[f]ar from the subject-object relation being constitutive of knowledge, the existence of a subject and an object is the first and major illusion of knowledge.' This image of truth, and accordingly this illusion of knowledge – which is in any case different from how we encounter truth in politics – came to prevail in science and played its part in dichotomizing power and knowledge.[5]

In contrast to the image of truth-sky, that of truth thunderbolt/lightening is important for getting at Foucault's political undertaking. This is so because it focuses on relations among people in the political community instead of through the lenses of the 'illusion of knowledge'. The image of truth-thunderbolt sees truth in relation to events, rituals, power, hunting and strategy, which links up with Foucault's experimental attitude where curiosity, boldness, courage and resolve play a major role. It, moreover, supports his focus on the truth-teller and his/her interlocutor in the political realm. For inasmuch as truth in politics is seen as a 'technology of demonstrative truth joined ... to scientific practice' (PP: 236), *political practice cannot avoid being crippled and liberty rendered impossible* as this technology is organized around the distinctions of true/false and subject/object, and is geared to reproduce what is 'universally present'. Insofar as this logic of demonstrative truth colonizes the 'mental horizon' of politics, and hence patterns of political interaction, political practice will inevitably succumb to an objectivity, which does not follow a political logic, but is geared to hierarchy and submission (Veyne 2010: 93–4). This will, moreover, tend to alienate the freedom associated with *parrhesia*.

By emphasizing that truth in politics is not the same as demonstrative truth, Foucault takes issue with emancipatory discourses associated with Marxism for not having been able to question the link between politics and demonstrative truth; and what is more relevant today, he questions the increased role of experts of all kinds in politics and public life in general. One might wonder whether the anti-political stance of emancipation as conceived by the Marxist tradition of scientific socialism was not directly linked to this notion of demonstrative truth and the concomitant neglect of power as governing. This might be so because the objectivity and universality of truth was incompatible with the subjectivity and partiality of power in which case liberation from domination would entail an escape from politics. From Foucault's perspective such an escape from politics could not be liberating as the very means of emancipation is the set-up of an alienating truth regime, which is antithetic to liberty as, precisely, a political practice.

Finally, it is worth noting the differences between Foucault's argument concerning the specificity and autonomy of politics and those in the Marxist traditions who also argue that politics and political power have some kind of autonomy. One of the differences between Foucault and Marxists, Postmarxist, Poststructuralists, and the like, is that for Foucault the autonomy of political power and the political field is a *project* as opposed to be either an epiphenomenon or an ontologically privileged part of reality. It is, in other words, a task or a strategy, because it belongs to the order of what happens, which means that it is inseparable from struggles for democracy and individuality. It is, as I have argued, a political practice directed against religious forces, social elites and experts setting the political agenda. With this experiential approach, which is framed by the triangle of power, knowledge and ethics, and guided by a critical ethos as well as a deep resentment against hierarchy and obedience, Foucault differs significantly from those other strands of political and social theory in so-called radical traditions for whom the specificity and autonomy of politics – or rather 'the political' – are asserted axiomatically, who have an epistemological approach to critique and make a virtue of 'demonstrative truth', and whose critical sense has been systematically one sided.

Parrhesia: communal life vs hierarchy and obedience

In contrast to rhetoric, one of the functions of *parrhesia* is that it is a transmission of truth where one 'speaks to the other in such a way that this other will be able to form an autonomous, independent, full and satisfying relationship to himself' (HS: 379, see also 382). This is a power relation, which facilitates and develops one's abilities to govern oneself and others, and which does not hinge on the 'power over' model as it does not involve domination. This implies that the figure of power/resistance, in which freedom ensures that one does not end up in a state of domination, withdraws in favour of another view of power/critique in relation to government. Here, the context is that of political authority. Foucault does not assume that power is exercised only to assert one's self-interest or will against that of others, but emphasizes that power in a democracy can facilitate people's autonomy and conditions of life (HS: 379, 385). This is yet another indication that the moral commitment of *parrhesia* is generosity. This should be understood in a political sense and not merely as a personal quality of the one engaging in *parrhesia*. It is a political virtue because it is geared to common concerns as opposed to being guided by personal gain, and because it focuses attention on what is the best thing to do in situations based on criteria of reasonability and trustworthiness. It is important to keep in mind that this does not rule out that the parrhesiast is a politically engaged person who takes an interest in what is going on. On the contrary, the parrhesiast is not a detached expert, be that a philosopher or a technocrat, but is part of the political community and takes part in it as a citizen among others.

Parrhesia is a democratic bonding between free and equal citizens and the political community of which they are part of. It 'only exists when there is freedom in the enunciation of the truth, freedom of the act by which the subject says the truth, and freedom also of the pact by which the subject speaking binds himself to the statement and enunciation of the truth.' *Parrhesia* is accordingly 'the free courage by which one binds oneself in the act of telling the truth...*parresia* is the ethics of truth-telling as an action which is risky and free' (both GSO: 66; see also HS: 411 note 28). The function of truth-telling in politics is to ascertain the seriousness of the citizen speaking on behalf of, or as a critic of, political authorities and suggesting a particular course of action, which requires personal integrity and courage as it might be risky. To tell the truth links up with duty: one is free either to speak or to remain silent, but one feels obligated to tell the truth. By voluntarily doing that, one has to be prepared to bear the costs, which is why *parrhesia* is linked up with personal integrity, freedom and courage. 'The orator who speaks the truth', says Foucault (FS: 19), 'to those who cannot accept his truth, for instance, and who may be exiled, or punished in some way, is *free* to keep silent. No one forces him to speak, but he feels that it is his duty to do so.' So, the parrhesiastic pact, which binds the individual to his/her statement as well as to the community, is one that is entered freely, and it is this freedom which is the basis for speaking of duty. Duty does not then entail obedience (WC: 49).

To approach duty in this way is diametrically opposed to authoritarian and reactionary critics of democracy for leading to governmental mediocrity and disorder. This criticism centres on the problem of obedience, which is a problem of upholding hierarchical political structures that are able to control people and lock them into a state of subordination by monitoring and disciplining them vigilantly. It is this problem of trying to restore or maintain hierarchical authority that is, says Foucault (CT: 336), 'at the heart of this reversal of the values of *parrhesia*'. And, he goes on, '[w]here there is obedience there cannot be *parrhesia*'. This is so because the 'classical' understanding of *parrhesia* was that it was a right and a privilege for the citizen to express his views and to partake in collective decision-making (CT: 34). *Parrhesia* means to tell the truth without concealment and the parrhesiastic pact between the one who speaks and his/her interlocutor consists in 'the courage of truth in the person who speaks and who ... takes the risk of telling the whole truth that he thinks' and 'the interlocutor's courage in agreeing to accept the hurtful truth that he hears' (CT: 13, see also 142–3). To engage in this game, and to enter this pact, is only possible on the basis of a fundamental political equality between citizens, which again signals that the power of political authorities is not founded on hierarchy and the domination that goes with it. Political authority cannot then be equated with legitimate domination, as mainstream political science/sociology would have it.

The power of authority does not entail domination just as it does not have to be legitimated by reference to, for example, a constitutional set-up or popular consent. What Foucault's discussions of *parrhesia* give way for is the insight that the relationship between authorities and non-authorities in a political community does not need to be a hierarchical one marked by domination, obedience and so forth. It merely states a difference between the few who make decisions and the many that do not. *Parrhesia* holds a door open for the option, however unlikely, that those who exercise political power are guided by what they reasonably conceive as the best thing to do and that they do not manipulate to get their way. What matters is that if one rejects that this is possible by definitional fiat, the only alternative to repressive power politics is to indulge in anti-politics, be that the cynical introversion of the ironic commentator or the totalitarian ideological fantasies of emancipation.

At this junction one should note that for Foucault equality and communal life are inseparable from personal integrity and freedom. In his very last lecture Foucault elaborates on how the meaning of *parrhesia* was transformed in early Christianity. It was transformed from a horizontal relationship between citizens in the democratic city-state to a vertical one between the individual and God. Within the latter there is an early and a later meaning of *parrhesia*. In the earlier version associated with Christian mysticism, the term still retained a positive core because one could be 'in *parrhesia* with God: openness of heart, immediate presence, and direct communication of the soul and God' (CT: 333, see also 326–7). This state of confidence forms the basis of amongst other things the 'courageous boldness' of the martyr, the parrhesiast par excellence (CT: 332). *Parrhesia* is then a relationship to others rooted in the relationship of trust in God.

However, with the development of a clerical hierarchy and its ideology of a God to be feared, the 'theme of *parrhesia*-confidence will be replaced by the principle of a trembling obedience, in which the Christian will have to fear God and recognize the necessity of submitting to His will, and to the will of those who represent Him' (CT: 333). When individuals must entrust the conduct of their soul to pastors, priests or bishops in hierarchical institutions (CT: 333), that is, when their relationship with God has to be mediated by others to whom they have to show obedience, it follows that they cannot bring about their salvation by themselves. On the contrary, when the individual 'can have it only through the intermediary of these structures of authority, then this is in fact the sign that he must mistrust himself' (CT: 334). 'He must', Foucault goes on, 'be the object of his mistrust. He must be the object of an attentive, scrupulous, and suspicious vigilance' (CT: 334). What we see here is the final showdown of *parrhesia*, because the term, according to Christian orthodoxy, or rather to the imperatives of a repressive religious/political authority, connotes everything that is evil: that one has confidence in oneself and others, as well as 'in what can be done together' (CT: 335); that one, accordingly, engages on par with others in communal life and that one accepts 'what they do and say' (CT: 336). *Parrhesia* is identified with familiarity with the world and with 'non-fear of God, non-mistrust of self, and non-mistrust of the world', all of which is now seen as arrogance, which one must turn away from (CT: 336).

It has, needless to say, major implications for political life that individuals' trust in self and others is supplanted by mistrust and fear. What is at stake is the very quality of the political culture. Interaction amongst equals vanishes and instead comes hierarchy and commands and their corollary, subservience and a culture of dependency; free speech is censored by others and/or by oneself with the result that 'courageous boldness' vanishes; individuality and reciprocal acceptance of differences are replaced by conformity just as a vibrant culture of political engagement dies and indifference and hypocrisy become the order of the day.

Notes

1 It is beyond the scope of this book to deal with the affinities between the later Foucault and the later Rawls. Here it will suffice to refer to the few who have probed the thematic links between them, notably Fleischacker 2013: chs 9–10; Moss 1998; Patton 2010 and Redhead 2010.

2 'I think that the theoretical opposition between the state and civil society, on which political theory has been labouring for a hundred and fifty years, is not very productive', says Foucault, IF: 290. Villadsen and Dean (2012: 402–4) try to explain away Foucault's critique of this opposition by reducing his comments to the contexts of polemical exchanges in the late 1970s. In my opinion, this is not a viable, let alone fruitful, way of getting at Foucault's argument, which, instead, should be seen in the context of carving out the specificity and autonomy of politics. This is especially clear in Foucault's lecture on civil society in *The Birth of Biopolitics*, which is transformed from a legal to a political concept with the rise of the political economy. Juridical theory with its subject of rights is inadequate to govern a space of sovereignty inhabited by economic subjects. Civil society becomes a politicized space generated by liberal governmental technologies (BB: 294–7), and government becomes an organic component of the social bond just as the social bond becomes an organic feature of the form of authority (BB: 308).

3 Rawls 1995: 174–5. This argument is closely related to the principle that preconditions democracy, namely the autonomy of politics, relies on the bracketing of social factors that undermine the principle of liberty and equality. The point is also that whilst technical expertise is recognized as important, it is mandatory for democracy that political matters are dealt with by everybody in their capacity as citizens (Saxonhouse 2006: 94).

4 It should be noted that Foucault speaks of prophecy, wisdom, teaching, technique and *parrhesia* as five fundamental and partially overlapping modes of truth-telling. The political mode (*parrhesia*) cannot then be insulated from the other ones (CT: 26–7). This does not, however, prevent the democratic project from aiming *parrhesia* to be 'freestanding' in relation to prophecy, wisdom and so on.

5 Cf. Foucault's comments on positivism ten years earlier that knowledge of madness was based on the medical profession's ability to master it (HM: 505–6).

7
Leadership and Community: Critique of Obedience and Democratic Paradoxes

Abstract: *The chapter focuses on the paradoxes of democratic governmentality, which take off from to the tension between differentiation and ascendency introduced by* parrhesia *and the democratic ethos of equality. The argument of Plato as well as twentieth century elitists is that democracy leads to government failure and fragmentation of the polity. Truth-telling in a democracy is impossible because the majority principle implies that the few who are insightful and capable are subjected to the many that are ignorant and incapable. Foucault takes issue with these elitist arguments, which strike at the core of democratic governmentality, whilst at the same time acknowledging democratic paradoxes related to* parrhesia. *Foucault's approach is able to address the reactionary criticisms of democracy whilst acknowledging the reality of these paradoxes.*

Keywords: agonism; democratic paradoxes; elitism; ethical differentiation

Dyrberg, Torben Bech. *Foucault on the Politics of Parrhesia*. Basingstoke: Palgrave Macmillan, 2014.
DOI: 10.1057/9781137368355.0009.

Parrhesia and/or democracy?

In this chapter I will continue the discussion of *parrhesia* in relation to public political reasoning by focusing on democratic dilemmas and paradoxes related to the leadership/community relationship. The chapter begins with Foucault's interrogation of the essential elitist assumption from Plato onwards that the rationale of government must be based on domination/obedience. I then move on to discuss a double paradox of democracy caused by the tension between differentiation and ascendency introduced by *parrhesia* and the democratic ethos of equality.

Foucault looks at Plato's criticism of democracy as necessarily resulting in governmental failure and fragmentation of the polity. This criticism is formulated as a strong reservation against *parrhesia*, which will, inevitably, according to Plato, degenerate into rhetoric and flattery, as the bulk of the population is easy to manipulate due to its ignorance and inclination to be led by narrow self-interests. The argument we find in Plato, as well as in twentieth-century elitist traditions, is that democracy is confronted with an insurmountable governmentality problem, which orbits around the structural impossibility that 'the very form of democracy cannot leave any place for truth-telling' (CT: 45). The reason is that the majority principle of democracy precludes 'ethical differentiation', because the few who are insightful and capable are subjected to the many that are ignorant and incapable of distinguishing between good and bad.

It is significant that Foucault took issue with these elitist arguments, which strike at the core of democratic governmentality. This is yet another indication that his enquiry differs from most others who consider themselves radical or critical, but who have not taken issue with the assumptions of elitism. One of the major reasons is that the self-professed radicals have, in fact, inherited these very assumptions, which were dealt with in the first chapter: that politics and power are equated with conflict and domination, respectively, and that political power is a matter of struggles between vested interests and identity formations. When democracy is structured around this skeleton, it is no wonder that liberalism as normative theory and ideology can only envision human flourishing at a distance from politics, just as it comes as no surprise that emancipation in Marxism is envisioned as an end of politics, which simply takes this anti-political maxim one step further by elimination politics altogether. Foucault refers to this flight from political power when he mentions that the socialist tradition never developed an understanding of governmentality. As a result, it could not be 'the alternative to liberalism' (BB: 94), because it could not match the rationality of the liberal art of government in which 'the rationality of the governed must serve as the regulating principle for the rationality of government', so as to found 'the principle of rationalization of the art of government on the rational behavior of those who are governed' (BB: 312).

Democracy and the problem of ethical differentiation

How is it possible to deal with authoritarian, reactionary or elitist criticisms of democracy that *parrhesia* or truth-telling is impossible in democracy for a structural reason, namely that it is incapable of ethical differentiation? Democracy is not, so the critique goes, able to differentiate true from false, good from bad and so on, because governors and governed change roles, decisions are made by majority vote, which implies that they are liable to be the outcome of popular moods and marked by sectional interests. Other regime forms, aristocratic or monarchic, for instance, are not exempt from problems related to truth-telling, but the kind of danger confronting these regimes is tyranny – that the ruler turns out to be a tyrant who is ill-tempered and bad mannered and hence not up to the task of being told the truth. The inevitable result is bad government and oppression. The criticism of democracy from Plato and Aristotle onwards goes roughly like this: as opposed to monarchy and aristocracy, democracy is especially exposed to suffer from bad *parrhesia*, that is to say, flattery and rhetoric subdue truth-telling because it is easy to manipulate the many who are neither informed nor cultivated and who are not able to take the long view and the view that benefits the city or the state, as they are prone to follow their narrow here-and-now interests and inclinations.[1] The point is not that true discourse in itself is powerless, meaning that the real issue is not a question of truth vs power, but that truth is rendered contextually powerless due to the structure of democracy. This is so, says Foucault (CT: 40), because 'in democracy one cannot distinguish between good and bad speakers, between discourse which speaks the truth and is useful to the city, and discourse which utters lies, flatters, and is harmful.' Again, the result is poor government performance and fragmentation of the polity.

The elitist and reactionary arguments that these governmentality problems are most pronounced in democracy are expressed at two levels. The first one deals with appearances, namely that the parrhesiast is 'the impenitent chatterbox, someone who cannot restrain himself or, at any rate, someone who cannot index-link his discourse to a principle of rationality and truth' (CT: 9–10). To grant 'freedom of speech to everyone risks mixing up true and false, favoring flatterers, and exposing those who speak to personal dangers'. The second concerns the 'more fundamental, structural impossibility' that 'the very form of democracy cannot leave any place for truth-telling' (CT: 44–5). The reason is that the few who are better are subjected to the many that are worse, because the values have been reversed. To argue on those lines captures a conservative insight: that democracy, which is founded on the autonomy of political practice, represents a political reversal of the traditional cultural values and the institutionalized hierarchies they underpin, and that the unavoidable consequence of this 'ideological' assault on culture is disorder and ungovernability. In other words, individuals are not free and equal. On the contrary, liberty and equality is a democratic artifice based on the autonomy of politics.

For a political constructionist such as Foucault, democratic political order is a construction, an act of will as opposed to fate, which cannot rely on pre-political and hence comprehensive views concerning, for example, social stratification, gender and ethnicity. Democracy thus conceived is fragile and there are structural reasons why truth-telling is precarious, because the power/knowledge/ethics triangle cannot be anchored in something beyond questioning. However, that it is doomed to failure is far from obvious, which should be clear when discussed from the vantage point of public political reasoning such as Foucault's *parrhesia*. It is vital to acknowledge that there is a problem, but then again, other regime forms are also fragile and the precariousness of truth in relation to power is by far just a democratic problem. However, that does not mean that these reactionary arguments can be swept aside as being just a straw man put up to legitimate the privileges of the few against the many. There is a problem and the question is how to deal with it, well knowing that there is no unique solution, which will solve all problems.

Public political reasoning and *parrhesia* form part of a political account of democratic government, and they contribute to cope with the problems raised by reactionary critics that democracy is especially prone to suffer from, say, manipulation, bad leadership, the prevalence of partial interests and fragmentation. Public political reasoning is a way of conducting oneself and the interaction of people when it comes to deal with matters of common concerns. Its status as freestanding implies that community life is approached in such a way that one's moral, religious and such ways of reasoning are put between brackets. Public reason is a way of dealing with differences of conviction, interests and opinions that make it unacceptable to extrapolate non-public reasons to the public domain. This implies three things, which can be categorized in Foucault's triangle of power, knowledge and ethics.

First the dimension of power, namely that community life is shielded from the forces of, notably, religious, nationalist or racist doctrines, which are all strong poles of identification. This means that they are rallying points for a high degree of political intensity, which in turn make them divisive factors that might easily fragment or tear a community apart. This is the topic of what is included on the political agenda and what is excluded. The point is, on the one hand, that the non-public status of comprehensive doctrines means that they have no veto power in politics and, on the other, that it is unacceptable to exclude citizens on the basis of comprehensive outlooks such as sexist or racist ones.

The second dimension is knowledge, which is that public reason gears interaction towards issues at hand, which are of common concern as opposed to take over an agenda dictated from the outside by, for example, experts. To do that would undermine the autonomy of politics and degrade political deliberation and representation thus turning politics into a mere effect of external forces. To deal with issues in a political light implies that it is possible to approach them somewhat differently as they are no longer ingrained in comprehensive views, as it were. This will make it easier to engage in compromises and to conduct interaction according to criteria of soberness and a sense of detachment, which makes it more likely that decisions are well prepared and digested.

Third, the dimension of ethics concerns the formation of the individual taking part in political interaction. Given that public reasoning is a way of arguing and comporting oneself, which construes political interaction as freestanding, it becomes, nonetheless, possible for individuals engaging in discussions or agonistic strife to put themselves in the place of the other to make an informed and balanced judgement (cf. Arendt 1968). This bracketing what is personal and/or non-public is made possible first because individuals are politically equal, just as they are free in the sense of taking responsibility for their actions and for speaking out as opposed to be subdued or to subdue themselves. Freedom of expression is an obvious case and the bottom-line of *parrhesia*, which speaks out against both censorship and self-censorship.

These three aspects of public political reasoning – power, knowledge and ethics – have a stabilizing effect on government, which work against fragmentation, manipulation and ill-considered decisions. They can be seen as forming governmentality, that is, political ways of governing which in varying degrees involve these three dimensions. It is important to note the temporal and spatial aspects at work here: the temporal dimension means that public political reasoning is cultivated in a political community over long stretches of time and solidly rooted in civic traditions. This is what Rawls (1993: 54, 157) refers to as political capital ingrained in ordinary social relations. The spatial dimension indicates that public reason connects political culture and political decision-making. In other words, it links political authorities to the political community at large. Both of these dimensions tend to prevent the formation of a political class insulated from ordinary citizens. This makes it more difficult to establish hierarchical institutions, which thrive on a culture of dependency and subservience. It seems likely that the main target of Foucault's critical encounters is a political culture of obedience regardless of whether it is enforced by, say, sovereign, disciplinary or bio-political power. If such a culture is the flip side of elite rule, then there is a self-fulfilling prophecy involved in the latter's assumption of the political stupidity of the vast majority of the population. For the civic dignity, that goes hand in hand with a vibrant political culture, in which *parrhesia* is an integral part, has been wiped out in a political culture marked by conformity and collective mediocrity.

Parrhesia and democratic paradoxes

The political way to get political power accepted by free and equal citizens in a democracy is based on the premise that it is crucial for people – and defining popular sovereignty – how one convinces others and the extent to which one keeps one's words and sticks to one's decisions. Whether explanations of events, trends, conflicts, and so on, are true or false, or whether the suggested courses of action are appropriate are, needless to say, important. However, the bottom-line framing political interventions is that political actors operating in public political forums are ready to argue their case in terms of common concerns. Thus by filtering comprehensive views Foucault's argument is similar to Rawls' (1993: 241) when he holds that public reason ask us 'to conduct our fundamental discussions in terms of what we regard as a political conception'. The point is that in a democracy, societal coexistence has to be framed politically by bracketing extra-political sources of authority related to the triangle of power, knowledge and ethics, alias social stratification, demonstrative truth and comprehensive ethical doctrines.

In making this move, Foucault connects the discussion of democracy centred on liberty and equality at the input side with a discussion of what conditions a political authority that seeks to neither manipulate people's opinions nor control their lives by keeping them in a state of subordination and dependence. On the contrary, the leitmotif for the kind of political power, which is shaped vis-à-vis *parrhesia*, is that the one who speaks does so freely and courageously, and the one who listens develops an ability to conduct him/herself in order to conduct the behaviour of others. This is to suggest that there are both political and moral dimensions of *parrhesia*, which are closely linked (HS: 385).

On the one hand, it is critical that one tells others the truth about how they can make use of politically communicated messages to develop their abilities and govern themselves and others in ways which will improve their everyday life. On the other hand, this message ought to be guided by generosity rather than selfishness, which is, as mentioned, the kernel of the political virtue to the other in *parrhesia*. But there is something more to generosity, which has to do with power and autonomy, and which looks at how it is possible to link democracy and *parrhesia* when exercising political power. If power in general and political power in particular were inherently negative, that is, a means to subdue and manipulate others, this link would not make any sense, because *parrhesia* then would have to be defined in anti-political terms, that is, as a flight from politics. The political power Foucault has in mind, however, is one that aims to get others to do what they might not otherwise have done, wanted to do or been able to do, by telling them the truth as it appears here and now, and seen from the perspective of a reasonable and visionary political authority. This is clear, for example, in Foucault's statement (HS: 384; see also GSO: 179) that *parrhesia* is a particular practice of true discourse defined by rules of prudence, skill, and the conditions that require one to say the truth at this moment, in this form, under these conditions, and to this individual inasmuch, and only inasmuch as he is capable of receiving it best, at this moment in time.

Two things are important here. First, it should be clear that we are not dealing with a detached or impartial observer, which would be the image of the 'philosophical expert', but with a trustworthy, rational and generous person who is part of 'the political game'. Second, while *parrhesia* is engrained in a situational logic by being geared to the event and to say the right thing at the right moment, it also exceeds the momentary as it is a political type of communication that takes long and sustained training.

It follows that parrhesiastic generosity is a practice of caring for the other, which is geared to enhancing the other's autonomy. While this holds as a general parrhesiastic maxim – meaning both in political and, for instance, educational contexts – things look somewhat different in relation to democracy, where the difference between good and bad *parrhesia* is on the agenda (GSO: 168, 180–1, 200). The danger of *parrhesia* is that this way of governing democracy is a difficult art of striking a balance between, on the one hand, to exercise powers generously and on the basis of sound judgement, and on the other, to advance one's partial interests by way of flattery and rhetoric thus appealing to popular trends and sentiments. The battle of democracy is a matter of good vs bad *parrhesia*; that is, the question is whether democracy underpins the 'distinctive difference of truth-telling in the game of democracy' (GSO: 183) or, as Plato holds, it does the opposite by allowing both the best and the worst to speak in consequence of which *parrhesia* degenerates to 'ignorant outspokenness' deprived of intellectual and moral qualities (FS: 73, see also 66–7). This would tend to fragment the political community by appealing to the 'superfluous desires' of the many by flattering them (GSO: 200, see also 301). At stake here is the issue of what true discourse does to democracy, which concerns how the ethos of equality is related to the making of difference. With reference to the relationship between *isegoria* and *parrhesia*, Foucault states (GSO: 183; see also Saxonhouse 2006: 94–6):

> On the one hand in fact, there can only be true discourse, the free play of true discourse, and access to true discourse for everybody where there is democracy. However, and this is where the relationship between true discourse and democracy becomes difficult and problematic, it has to be

understood that true discourse is not and cannot be distributed equally in a democracy according to the form of *isegoria*. Not everybody can tell the truth just because everybody may speak. True discourse introduces a difference or rather is linked, both in its conditions and in its effects, to a difference: only a few can tell the truth.

Thus conceived, it will be necessary to differentiate between democracy at the entrance to the political scene (*isegoria*) and the communication of true discourses at the exit when policies are being delivered (*parrhesia*). The legitimate exercise of power in a democracy depends on true discourses where the couplet power/knowledge is not conceived in terms of domination but as political ways of reasoning in public. However, not everybody possesses the knowledge, experience and vision required to take up the role of a political authority, and has the ability and the courage to tell the truth irrespective of whether people want to hear it. If the only ones who can do that are the few, who are especially gifted in the political sense of the term, it cannot avoid creating problems for democratic principles and ambitions concerning equality. The true discourse of the few is a condition for maintaining and developing democracy in the same way as democracy, as everybody's free and equal access to and recognition in the decision-making process, is a precondition for a true discourse to come about and take form in political governing.

In discussing *parrhesia* vis-à-vis democracy, we come across a double paradox. The first is that true and reasonable discourse is conditioned by, and conditions, democracy, because this is the only acceptable way of getting free and equal individuals to obey political authorities and to co-exist in the political community. However, as it is only very few who have the intellectual and moral ability and the guts to tell the truth and hold on to it, *parrhesia* cannot but introduce a political dimension, which fits uneasily with the democratic ethos of equality. The question is how to deal with the paradox that although citizens are free and equal there are, however, some who are able to ascend over others when it comes to exercising political power (FS: 72–3, 77, 82). More to the point, because democracy as any other regime form requires leadership, constitutionally granted liberty and equality have to be supplemented by intellectual, political, social and moral qualities, which cannot be institutionally defined. *Parrhesia* is the name for these qualities supplementing democracy. This supplementary status implies that *parrhesia* does not produce codified effects but instead 'opens up an unspecified risk' (GSO: 62), which is inscribed in democracy. *Parrhesia* itself is also at risk as it might degenerate into manipulation and flattery, part of the reason being that it might adopt rhetoric to persuade; yet the mere purpose of persuasion must not overshadow the prime virtues of *parrhesia* of accuracy and sincerity, which make up truthfulness (Williams 1996: 603, 607).

The second paradox consists in the risk, which is closely linked to the 'dynamic and agonistic structure of *parresia*' (GSO: 156) characterizing a democracy and which is, moreover, the best guarantee for true and courageous discourse to prevail. The paradox consists in the risk that *parrhesia* degenerates by being contaminated by rhetoric, flattery and demagoguery because political authorities need to shape public opinion and ward off criticism. In other words, to be frank and to take risks are not sufficient to disclose the truth (FS: 73), and this means that *parrhesia* becomes a means to achieve or maintain political power, or to prevent others from doing it. True and courageous discourse, which were vehicles of democracy, then turn into its opposite and becomes a mere rhetorical figure, because that which conditioned it has rendered it powerless (GSO: 184; Hardt 2010: 156–7). The idea of discussing these dilemmas and paradoxes is to pinpoint Foucault's attentiveness to the political challenges facing relations between authorities and laypeople in a democracy. In contrast to elitist and critical traditions, I will argue that a Foucauldian approach is able to address reactionary criticisms of democracy whilst acknowledging dilemmas and paradoxes of democratic governability.

When individuals speak frankly and engage with political authorities, they say what they truly consider being right or to be the best thing to do. In this respect, the parrhesiast aims for political power by trying to convince others. They hereby take upon themselves the task and the responsibility to govern the political community, which unavoidably involves disagreement and conflict. This is the reason Foucault (GSO: 156) speaks of 'a superiority shared with others, but shared in the form of competition, rivalry, conflict, and duel'. This is what characterizes the political game (*dunasteia*) 'as a field of experience with its rules and normativity' (GSO: 159), which is different from constitution and law (*politeia*). Dunasteia is about exercising power in conflict with others. It is related to ascendency and designates 'the exercise of power, or the game through which power is actually exercised in a democracy ... *Dunasteia* is the problem of the political game, of its rules and instruments, and of the individual who engages in it.' (GSO: 158).

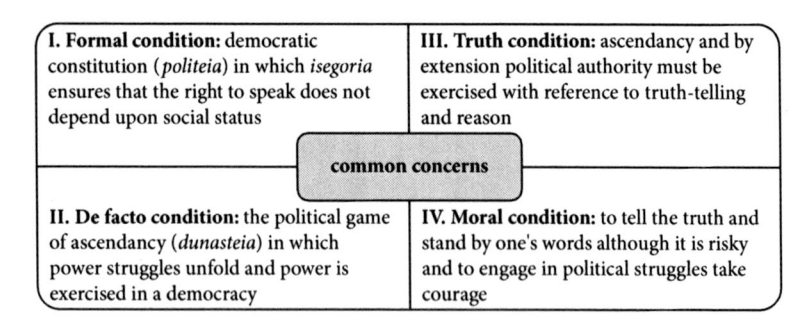

I. Formal condition: democratic constitution (*politeia*) in which *isegoria* ensures that the right to speak does not depend upon social status	**III. Truth condition:** ascendancy and by extension political authority must be exercised with reference to truth-telling and reason
common concerns	
II. De facto condition: the political game of ascendancy (*dunasteia*) in which power struggles unfold and power is exercised in a democracy	**IV. Moral condition:** to tell the truth and stand by one's words although it is risky and to engage in political struggles take courage

FIGURE 7.1   *The framing of* parrhesia

Foucault's mentioning of the *parrhesia* circuit or the rectangle of *parrhesia* emphasizes exactly this difference between law and power. *Parrhesia* links *politeia* and *dunasteia* (I and II in Figure 7.1), and it is at this meeting point that we find 'the root of a problematic of a society's immanent power relations which, unlike the juridical-institutional system of that society, ensure that it is actually governed' (GSO: 159). In other words, *parrhesia* relies on the right to speak (*isegoria*), which is granted by the formal condition of the democratic constitution, but it adds something. 'It is what allows some individuals to be among the foremost, and, addressing themselves to the others, to tell them what they think, what they think is true ... by telling the truth, to persuade the people with good advice, and thus direct the city and take charge of it' (GSO: 157–8). What is at stake in the discussion of *parrhesia* is the nature of the political game and the quality of democratic government. The stakes could not be higher! This signals the importance Foucault attaches to *parrhesia*, which is constituted by the four corners in the rectangle:

The *parrhesia* circuit is about how to cope with the apparent paradox that even though every citizen is free and equal there are, nonetheless, somebody in charge. Some people are able to ascend over others and exercise political power in agonistic confrontations. The question is then how they can do that on democratic ground. The more general question is what democratic political authority is all about.

There are two conditions political agents should honour to be able to exert power on democratic ground. First, they have to engage in true discourses as they are perceived from their perspective in a given situation (HS: 384), and in the context of agonistic encounters. Contestation is vital because the competition between several voices makes it more likely that people make an informed choice, which is to say that it alleviates the democratic problem of how to differentiate between those who are capable of governing from those who are not. In addition, it puts the sincerity of the speaker to a test, which makes flattery and rhetoric less likely, which, again, facilitates the entering of the parrhesiastic pact where the individual binds him/herself to his/her word. Second, they have to show courage, resolution and solidarity with the political community and act in accordance with its common interests in light of the risks, dangers and challenges confronting it. Foucault talks about political agents acting in the name of the values and interests of the political community – acts that at the same time partake in defining or reshaping these values and this community. In contrast to communitarian discourses, these values are not defined prior to, or at a distance from, politics as pre-political norms, but are instead politically construed. It is not then a truth à la Habermas' regulative idea about the marginalization of power in the ideal speech situation. For in that case we would be dealing, partly, with a set-up that was imposed upon politics, and partly with a procedurally given set-up defining the conditions for legitimacy. We would, in other words, deal with an outside-in approach as opposed to one that is solidly placed in political interaction; just as it would be an input-driven approach in contrast to one that focuses on how political decisions and actions take effect and make a difference.

Parrhesia as demo-elitism?

In the light of Foucault's argument that *parrhesia* directly addresses political authorities and their critics, and that it historically was a concern for the top echelons of society only, it would perhaps be tempting to view *parrhesia* as a political communication and code of conduct among elites and sub-elites in which dissent is allowed (Brown 1992: ch. 2). Thus Foucault holds that *parrhesia* 'allows freedom to those who have to obey, or leaves them free at least insofar as they will only obey if they can be persuaded'. *Parrhesia*, he continues, 'persuades others whom one commands and which, in an agonistic game, allows freedom for others who also wish to command' as opposed to 'bending others to one's will' (GSO: 104, 105). Is this an elitist position or, more to the point, a demo-elitist one, which thrives on pluralism and for that reason exerts a more benign form of political domination? This is as far I can see questionable since there is no mentioning of hierarchies and the use of manipulation and coercion to uphold power, just as the focus on persuasion underscores reasonability, plurality and individual freedom.

There are two aspects here. The first one concerns the relationship between political authorities and their critics, which is the context of agonistic encounters. Here Foucault mentions (GSO: 135) that '[f]or the stronger to be able to govern reasonably ... the weaker will have to speak to the stronger and challenge him with her discourse of truth.' The second aspect concerns the nature of the political community as a whole, or more precisely, it looks at how regime structures influence political relations among laypeople/citizens. Here the emphasis is more on the nature of political capital, that is, whether these relations are marked by trust in self and others, toleration of differences, individual autonomy, and so forth.

However, everything depends, of course, on how one defines elitism. A democratically inclined version of elitism as we find in Etzioni-Halevy might accommodate Foucault on this point as elitism does not have to depend upon these types of repression in order to function. Something more specific and substantial is needed. According to Etzioni-Halevy (1993: 103), 'the autonomy of elites forms an overarching meta-principle' of democracy, which means that 'the relative autonomy of elites forms a large part of what the principles of democracy are really about'. The point is that elite rule and democracy are not only compatible, but they reinforce each other in that it is only the former that is able to cash in on the values and principles of the latter. Gone is the earlier explicit contempt for democracy, its impossibility and undesirability; gone is also the explicit cynical view of people and their alleged inability to reason politically. Demo-elitism fully endorses democracy; it is open-minded and flexible, emphasizes equality and liberty and so on. It is still elitist though maintaining that politics is not a proper concern for laypeople who have for all practical purposes no political existence. Hence politics is or has to be the exclusive business of elites, which can easily fit into a governance perspective of loosely coupled and more or less informal network.

So, in going back to Foucault, would it be reasonable to describe him as a demo-elitist because he pays much attention to the ability of the few to govern the multitude? It is clear from his lectures that the politics of truth-telling gives priority to political authorities to formulate and implement policies in a way that is trustworthy and accountable to the political community. This is clearly the strength of his argument. Besides, to focus on the necessity of leadership is not enough to label him as an elitist, because this leadership relies on free and equal citizens in the democratic political community. However, the weakness is that the political role of people often seem to boil down to how they react to what political authorities say and do, that is do they, at the end of the day, accept or reject their policies as authoritative? In this, it does look as if his argument has an elitist touch, because it neglects the capacities of laypeople to act politically. Yet, at other times – for instance, in his last lecture on 28 March 1984 – he puts strong emphasis on a vibrant, assertive and tolerant political culture. The political interaction we find here cannot be described simply as reflexes to how political authorities exercise power, as it has a specificity of its own and can make an impact on authorities.

Whilst the truth-telling of political authorities is geared to making government better to govern the population, the free speech of citizens is concerned with building political capital and expanding practices of freedom. Authorities and community are connected as they make up different parts of a democratic political community. In addition, Foucault makes it clear that '[p]*arresia* consists in making use of *logos* in the *polis-logos* in the sense of true, reasonable discourse, discourse which persuades, and discourse which may confront other discourse and will triumph only through the weight of its truth and the effectiveness of its persuasion.' And, he continues, '*parresia* consists in making use of this true, reasonable, agonistic discourse, this discourse of debate, in the field of the *polis*' (GSO: 105). Unless it is only elites who take part in debating political issues, this argument cannot sustain the demo-elitist assumption that elites should be the meta-principle of democracy, as Etzioni-Halevy would have it (1993: part III, 1997). Besides, power is not defined as forcing others against their will, overcoming conflicts of interests or bringing about a culturally defined common good. On the contrary, it is up to those who receive the authorities' communication whether they accept or reject it as trustworthy and truthful (GSO: 104–5); and to be able to do that is only possible on the basis of a strong political culture in which one shows trust in oneself and others, and thus takes part in acting together.

It is the link between political authorities and political community vis-à-vis regime structures, which are, above all, interesting in Foucault's arguments concerning *parrhesia*. He paid much attention to creative and enabling authorities who are able to respond to changing circumstances in novel ways and to grasp political opportunities at the right moment for the sake of simultaneously increasing the strength of the state and the population. And he also focused on the ability and creativity of individuals in the political community to take care of and to govern themselves in a context marked by equality as opposed to hierarchy, and liberty as opposed to domination. In this respect, it is notable that (1) truth-telling in politics, that is, the systematic political articulation of truths, which deals with the authorities and their critics, and (2) democracy which is bound up with the political practice of liberty and equality in the political community, are closely connected, although they will always be in an intrinsic tension with one another. Democracy presumes that everybody is able to speak and act for themselves and to act in concert and this type of politics will inevitably get into conflict with political authorities, but there would be little inclination for the latter to tell the truth, if it were not for citizens' ability to engage politically and practice their freedoms to hold authorities accountable for what they do.

If it is at all possible to speak of a meta-principle of democracy in Foucault's work, it is more likely a combination of the two major concerns, which can be extracted from his analyses of *parrhesia*. The first one frames politics as a particular type of practice and looks at the very condition for establishing political interaction and hence government as autonomous vis-à-vis its cultural environment (HS3: 87–94). This requires, as I have already argued, three types of exclusions: (1) that of social stratification and the politics of privilege, which give way for a meritocratic principle of ascendance and governing; (2) that of comprehensive doctrines, notably religious and moral ones, which allow public political reasoning to guide political interaction and assert the equal liberty of citizens and (3) that of demonstrative truth with its objectivism that makes politics the business of experts. The second concern is that of his egalitarian and anarchic individualism pinpointing liberty and equality as the vehicle of reflection and choosing, on the one hand, and good government, on the other. The point is that even though Foucault gears his discussions of *parrhesia* towards political leadership, his aim is to flesh out the kind of political authority underpinning a vibrant democracy. In other words, there need not be an inherent contradiction between leadership and citizenship although the relationship between them is a thorny one and easily corruptible.

The late Foucault's political and ethical analytics revolves around this double paradox of a democracy that undermines a truthful authority, and a truthful authority that undermines a democracy. This paradox can only be grasped from within the political game and from the perspective of the loose coupling between an input-oriented politics geared to making decisions and an output-oriented politics geared to acting in politically efficient and acceptable ways. The paradox does not minimize the importance of *parrhesia* for democracy, as the latter is the specific object of the former (Hardt 2010: 156). In any case, there is no alternative for free and equal citizens than to enrol in public political reasoning and to govern and be governed by true and trustworthy discourses. This argument has an affinity with Rawls' public reason, which also speaks on behalf of the political society, although Foucault, when mentioning the circular relation between democracy and *parrhesia*, emphasizes that they stand in a relation of tension to each other (GSO: 155).

The question is how to cope with the tension between (1) democracy at the entrance to politics where individual liberty and equality is guaranteed by the democratic set-up judicially, politically and publicly and (2) *parrhesia* at the exit where equality has been replaced by difference because some have been elevated above the rest of the citizen body by exercising power as political authorities. This question touches among other things upon whether we are witnessing what Foucault (GSO: 201) called 'the rightful ascendency of true discourse' or the opposite. In other words, does a political leadership's use of *parrhesia* go together with truthfulness and trustworthiness or has it degenerated to demagoguery, flattery and so on? This is perhaps *the* democratic dilemma, which cannot simply be done away with or solved as it pertains to the very institution of democracy. The dilemma can, however, be alleviated by emphasizing two democratic imperatives, which are closely entwined and are of critical importance for Foucault's discussions of critique and *parrhesia*. First, relations between political authorities and their critics must be marked by agonistic encounters in the political domain where it is framed by mutual acceptance of differences. This framing is decisive because it facilitates individual freedom and risk-taking, cultivates a sense of toleration in the political community and puts a strain on abuses of political power. At the same time it puts a lid on the conformist and totalitarian attitudes of the polemicist for whom dissent is unacceptable and who, accordingly, treat dissenters as enemies. This is the reason Foucault (PPP: 382) sees 'polemics as a parasitic figure on discussion and an obstacle to the search for the truth'. The focus on agonism taps into the second democratic imperative that the political community ought not to be a hierarchical one in which obedience and conformity reign. For in that case, agonistic encounters and the plurality of values, interests, life-forms and so forth, which sustain these encounters, would be reduced to be a prerogative for the top echelons of society. Instead, a vibrant and hence a non-conformist democracy is the one in which individuals have trust in themselves and each other, and this trust is the building block of political capital.

Note

1 Arguments such as these are echoed in, for example, J. S. Mill's description on the collective mediocrity of the masses, which formed the background of his preference for plural voting.

8
Political Perspectives: Authority and the Duality of Power, Politics and Politicization

Abstract: *The last chapter wraps up some of the discussions related to* parrhesia, *which I have dealt with in the preceding chapters. Particular emphasis is given to Foucault's understanding of 'the domain of politics', two levels of analysing power (force and power) as well as what Foucault means by political authority. In addition,* parrhesia *as a critical encounter is supplemented with Foucault's scattered remarks on what it means to speak of politicization and what the stakes are when politicizing something.*

Keywords: domain of politics; force/power; *parrhesia*; political authority; politicization

Dyrberg, Torben Bech. *Foucault on the Politics of Parrhesia.* Basingstoke: Palgrave Macmillan, 2014. DOI: 10.1057/9781137368355.0010.

Throughout this book I have argued that Foucault's discussions of *parrhesia* emphasize that the autonomy of politics is underpinned by three types of exclusions related to Foucault's triangle of power, knowledge and ethics. They concern (1) social stratification, states of domination, hierarchy and obedience; (2) demonstrative truth and expert/technical knowledge and (3) religious dogma and conformity. What we get, on the basis of these exclusions, is a political interaction among free and equal citizens, which is underpinned by *isonomia* and *isegoria*. This is the democratic take off for *parrhesia*. Democracy builds on the autonomy of politics, which is, as it were, its necessary but not sufficient condition. To govern a democracy, the dangerous supplement of *parrhesia* is needed, which cannot be boxed into or safeguarded by constitutionally guaranteed rights. Instead, it opens up an unspecified risk, as Foucault says, because it walks a tightrope balance between truthfulness and trustworthiness, on the one side, and manipulation and demagoguery on the other. In this respect *parrhesia* signals the Janus face of democracy: on the one hand, the possibility of the rightful ascendance of competent, visionary and prudent political authorities, and on the other, the danger of mediocre, narrow-minded and short-sighted authorities.

In this final chapter I will situate *parrhesia* in the context of the domain of politics. I will look at how Foucault differentiates between the political powers related to governing and exercising authority and the power and/or force relations engrained in all kinds of disciplinary and regulatory institutions. In addition, by drawing attention to these two levels, Foucault is able to pinpoint the nature of politicization and differentiate conformist and critical ways of politicizing issues. This is relevant for grasping the democratic and critical potentials of *parrhesia*, just as it fleshes out the dangers associated with free speech.

In dealing with the specificity and autonomy of politics, as well as how it is ingrained in social relations, it is interesting to look at what Hans Sluga has to say with regard to what Foucault could possibly have meant with terms such as political power relations, politics and politicization. Needless to say, with Foucault one never gets a clear-cut definition, so one will have to patch up a picture, which can make sense and which is in line with the previous arguments that situate Foucault as a political theorist.

Although Sluga (2011: 73–4) does not formulate it in exactly these terms, I take his point to be that Foucault operates with two analytical levels: there are the 'supervenient' relations of power whose objects are other power relations, and there are the 'non-supervenient' relations of power whose objects are individuals, populations and material things. The former are strategical and political in a sense the latter are not. Supervenient power relations are political, that is, a type of practice which comprises 'a more-or-less global strategy for co-ordinating and directing those relations', by which Foucault refers to 'the set of relations of force in a given society [which] constitutes the domain of politics'.[1] Two remarks follow: First, to speak of politics in those terms – of coordinating and directing the *set* of force relations in a society – draws attention to the exercise of power by political authorities, which have a dual function. On the one hand, they take upon themselves the task to speak in the name of society and hence to allocate values authoritatively for a society (Easton 1953: chs 4–5). Hereby they take part in shaping the complex totality of force relations. On the other hand, their task is to settle things, to make the final decision, and to operate in a particular way, which is different from the force, violence and submission mode characterizing non-supervenient settings, at least those which Foucault studied in his disciplinary period.

Second, politics as the power exercised by political authorities is located at the supervenient level whose objects are those other power relations that appear as force relations when seen from the receiving end of the relation in the vast variety of institutions. These institutions make up a substantial part of the domain of politics as they play a key role in governing individuals and populations. In addition, one could also say there is politics within institutions because they are governed by professionals – such as the doctors in medical institutions – who assert their role as authorities in relation to the patients (HM: 503–11). Authority relationships based on the power/knowledge matrix has a political dimension: internally in institutions as well as at the regime level dealing with global strategies. Politics thus conceived is akin to what Foucault would later discuss in terms of government and governmentality, which are overarching categories compared to where politics takes place.

The two types of power relations (supervenient and non-supervenient) link up with Foucault's distinction between power and force. How is one to understand his statement (THS: 189) that '[e]very relation of force implies at each moment a relation of power ... and every power relation makes a reference ... to a political field of which it forms a part'? This is complicated given the fact that Foucault up to this point often used 'force' and 'power' interchangeably, but if that were the case here too, the sentence would not make sense. Later on he insisted on setting them apart by treating them as polar opposites because they entailed the absence and presence of freedom, respectively. Needless to say, to approach the power/force issue from this angle would not make sense either. A sociological interpretation could run like this: force is associated with disciplinary technologies operating in all kinds of institutions. It is ubiquitous, anonymous and comes from everywhere, and it is systematic, normalizing and leads to productive submission. This is pretty much what other academic trends pass as 'structure'. Power, on the other hand, connotes some kind of agency with its stress on, for example, intention, calculation and resistance (HS1: 94–5). When seen from this perspective, power could operate on the basis of and in-between structures, which would be an approach in vogue at that time, that is, in the latter half of the 1970s.

However, a political interpretation strikes me as more to the point. Keeping in mind that force relations are those power relations whose objects are individuals, populations and material things, Foucault's argument that those relations imply power relations would suggest that they can only operate if they are coordinated and directed politically. Political authority is, in other words, needed as these force relations cannot coordinate and direct themselves automatically as a whole. It follows that to say that force implies power could be taken to mean that the two levels are connected via the mechanisms Foucault outlines in the four preliminary rules (HS1: 98–102). These are the rules of (1) the immanence between power and knowledge; (2) the continual variations of power/knowledge as matrices of transformations; (3) the double conditioning between local and general strategies and (4) the tactical polyvalences of discourses that join together segments of power and knowledge.

Whilst the power operating in institutions (force) works directly on the individual body through technologies of training and submission (THS: 186), the power of coordinating and directing those force relations is, as Foucault would say later on, a conduct of conduct, which implicitly refers back to the two levels of the domain of politics. In this light one could approach his later take on power as 'a way of acting upon an acting subject or acting subjects by virtue of their being capable of action. A set of actions upon other actions' (SP: 220). Here he is referring to the supervenient level of political power relations the object of which is those power (force) relations whose object is the mixture of individuals, peoples and things. At this level power and government are two sides of the same coin. Power is 'a way in which certain actions may structure the field of other possible actions' and governing is 'to structure the possible field of action of others', which in turn implies not only that those others are free to act but also that this freedom is essential for the power relationship (SP: 222, 221).

In line with the above political interpretation, one could understand the force/power distinction as one between (1) power relations in general, that is, as a broad term geared to capture the design and effects of behavioural modification, which might, but does not have to, rely on individual freedom; and (2) the power of political authority as a distinct type of political communication acting on behalf of society, which does rely on individuals who are able to act. The point with regard to the latter as Foucault discusses it here is that political authority does not essentially operate by way of violence/submission or manipulation/rhetoric for that matter. The latter is particularly relevant in relation to his later discussions of *parrhesia*. The point is not, of course, to eliminate violence and manipulation from politics by definitional fiat, but to argue that these forms of interaction cannot replace authoritative political communication, namely to act on behalf of society by directing and determining.

Another angle on the issue of force/power would be to focus on who is who in the power relation. The image of power as a force relationship suggests, as I have already hinted at, that it is seen from the receiving end of a power relation. In dealing with hospitals, prisons, schools and so forth, Foucault looks at institutions that are strictly hierarchical. Individuals are thoroughly and constantly monitored and controlled, and the code of conduct is command/obedience. In such a setting individual freedom and negotiations are not on the agenda and this implies that resistance takes the form of escape, disobedience and obstruction. Seen in this light and from the perspective of those who are exposed or subjected to disciplinary power it makes sense to speak of power in terms of force, which are ingrained in daily routines and the materiality of things (work processes, architecture, time schedules etc.). Moreover, to look at power/knowledge as the set-up, where knowledge is closely entwined with behavioural modification and social control, adds further weight to the technocratic layout of subject/object relations, and, as I discussed in Chapter 6, such an expert discourse rules out politics as encounters among equals and hence a democratic set-up.

Foucault's later interest in bio-politics, governmentality and, especially, *parrhesia* suggests two types of changes in his argument, which are closely related as they concern the nature of knowledge and the location of political power. The first is that he dissociates politics and political power from the technical knowledge of social control and mastery, and sees the former in the context of practical knowledge. In doing so, he gives way for a different take on politics and hence also critique and resistance, which in turn paves the way for the autonomy of politics and for *parrhesia* as truthful and trustworthy speech. The second point concerns his change of focus from the non-supervenient to the supervenient settings of power relations, and this implies that force as an image of power becomes both inadequate and misleading. Two types of contingency are at work here. One that stresses that this kind of power (force) is a specific type of power as opposed to providing an exhaustive characterization of power; and the other that a broad approach to power is formed and produce effects in relation to knowledge and ethics. It is through this triangle Foucault delineates the field of politics and modes of political subjectivation. These two changes, including the two types of contingency, frame his discussions of *parrhesia* as the type of communication existing between authorities and their critics as well as among laypeople in the political community. This underlines the twin-aspect of *parrhesia*: that it is a situational logic of having the guts to say the right thing at the right moment, and that it is a vital part of the political capital of a democratic political community.

Let me finally say a few words on politicization, which links Foucault's discussions of politics and political authority, on the one hand, and the critical aspirations of *parrhesia*, on the other. Politicization implies two things. First, that something becomes an issue of politics; that is, it is put on the political agenda and thus becomes a matter of coordination and direction of the whole. In a democracy this goes hand in hand with public political reasoning, accountability and transparency. The suggestion here is that politicization and democratization can be seen as two sides of the same coin, because that which is politicized has become an issue for political authorities and their critics. Second, politicization, as well as its opposite, depoliticization, takes place within the domain of politics, which includes both power and force. In contrast to both mainstream political science and the so-called radical approaches, politicization and depoliticization cannot be seen in terms of conflict and consensus, respectively, because politics and political power do not entail conflict and domination. Moreover, politicization does not encroach upon social relations from the outside, just as depoliticization is not the opposite, that is, a social logic imposing itself on what would otherwise count as political. The two levels are part of the domain of politics, which means that both politicization and depoliticization are strategies and tactics played out in this domain.

So, what we get here is three aspects of politicization: content, form and function. There is no a priori limits as to what can be politicized or depoliticized for that matter, which is to say that content implies that one sets out to politicize one thing rather than another and in one way or the other. The form concerns the choice between either 'to bring into being new schemas of politicization', for example, as an answer to 'the vast new techniques of power correlated with multinational economies and bureaucratic States' or 'falling back on ready-made choices and institutions', which is, according to Foucault not worthwhile (THS: 190). Politicization thus links up with the critical, timely and courageous facets of *parrhesia*. Finally, the function of politicization is to make certain relations of force the object of the 'more or less global strategies for co-ordinating and directing those relations', which Foucault spoke about above when describing political authorities (THS: 189). In doing so, they become an issue for political authorities making decisions concerning the allocation of values for a society.

Note

1 Foucault 1980: 189. In the first part of the quote Foucault speaks of 'directing'. This is the translation of the French 'finaliser', which indicates a type of practice that has the final say on a particular matter, in a word, an authority. In the second part of the quote the translation has been slightly modified. The English translation speaks of "the domain of the political". However, Foucault does not speak of "the political", but of "le domaine de la politique", that is, the domain of politics. See DE3: 233.

References

Abbreviations for works by Michel Foucault

Books

AK: *The Archaeology of Knowledge*, London: Tavistock 1972.

BB: *The Birth of Biopolitics*, Lectures at the Collège de France 1978–1979, Houndmills: Palgrave Macmillan 2008.

CT: *The Courage of Truth*, Lectures at the Collège de France 1983–1984, Houndmills: Palgrave Macmillan 2011.

EW2: *Aesthetics, Method, and Epistemology, The Essential Works of Michel Foucault 1954–1984*, Vol. 2, James D. Faubion (ed.), London: Penguin 1998.

EW3: *Power, The Essential Works of Michel Foucault 1954–1984*, Vol. 3, James D. Faubion (ed.), New York: The New Press 2000.

DE3: *Dits et écrits 1954–1988*, Vol. 3: 1976–1979, Paris: Gallimard.

DP: *Discipline and Punish: The Birth of the Prison*, New York: Vintage Books 1979.

FS: *Fearless Speech*, Joseph Pearson (ed.), Los Angeles: Semiotext(e) 2001.

GSO: *The Government of Self and Others*, Lectures at the Collège de France 1982–1983, Houndmills: Palgrave Macmillan 2010.

HM: *History of Madness*, Oxon: Routledge 2006.

References 127

HS: *The Hermeneutics of the Subject*, Lectures at the Collège de France 1981–1982, New York: Picador 2005.
HS1: *The History of Sexuality*, Vol. 1: *An Introduction*, London: Penguin 1981.
HS2: *The History of Sexuality*, Vol. 2: *The Use of Pleasure*, New York: Viking 1985.
HS3: *The History of Sexuality*, Vol. 3: *The Care of the Self*, London: Penguin 1990.
PP: *Psychiatric Power*, New York: Picador 2006.
RM: *Remarks on Marx*, Conversations with Duccio Trombarodi, New York: Semiotext(e) 1991.
SMD: *Society Must Be Defended*, Lectures at the Collège de France 1975–1976, London: Penguin 2004.
SW: *Sexualität und Wahrheit: Der Wille zum Wissen*, Frankfurt: Suhrkamp 1977.
WK: *Lectures on the Will to Know*, Lectures at the Collège de France 1970–1971, Houndmills: Palgrave Macmillan 2013.

Abbreviations for works by Foucault

Articles and interviews

BP: 'Body/Power', in Michel Foucault (1980), *Power/Knowledge: Selected Interviews and Other Writings 1972–1977*, Colin Gordon (ed.), New York: Pantheon Books, pp. 55–62.
CP: 'Candidacy Presentation: Collège de France, 1969', in Michel Foucault (1997), *Ethics: Subjectivity and Truth: The Essential Works of Michel Foucault 1954–1984*, Vol. 1, Paul Rabinow (ed.), London: Penguin, pp. 5–10.
ESF: 'The Ethics of the Concern for Self as a Practice of Freedom', in Michel Foucault (1997), *Ethics: Subjectivity and Truth, The Essential Works of Michel Foucault 1954–1984*, Vol. 1, Paul Rabinow (ed.), London: Penguin, pp. 281–301.
F: 'Foucault', in Michel Foucault (1998), *Aesthetics, Method, and Epistemology: The Essential Works of Michel Foucault 1954–1984*, Vol. 2, James D. Faubion (ed.), London: Penguin, pp. 459–63.
GE: 'On the genealogy of Ethics: An Overview of Work in Progress', in Michel Foucault (1997), *Ethics: Subjectivity and Truth,*

	The Essential Works of Michel Foucault 1954–1984, Vol. 1, Paul Rabinow (ed.), London: Penguin, pp. 253–80.
HN:	'Human Nature: Justice vs. Power, A Debate between Noam Chomsky and Michel Foucault', in Noam Chomsky and Michel Foucault (eds) (2006), *The Chomsky–Foucault Debate on Human Nature*, New York: The New Press and London: Routledge, pp. 1–67.
HOS:	'The Hermeneutics of the Subject', in Michel Foucault (1997), *Ethics: Subjectivity and Truth, The Essential Works of Michel Foucault 1954–1984*, Vol. 1, Paul Rabinow (ed.), London: Penguin, pp. 93–106.
IA:	'Interview with Actes', in Michel Foucault (2000), *Power, The Essential Works of Michel Foucault 1954–1984*, Vol. 3, James D. Faubion (ed.), New York: The New Press, pp. 394–402.
IF:	'Interview with Michel Foucault' by Duccio Trombadori, in Michel Foucault (2000), *Power, The Essential Works of Michel Foucault 1954–1984*, Vol. 3, James D. Faubion (ed.), New York: The New Press, pp. 239–97.
IT:	'So Is It Important to Think?' in Michel Foucault (2000), *Power, The Essential Works of Michel Foucault 1954–1984*, Vol. 3, James D. Faubion (ed.), New York: The New Press, pp. 454–8.
MP:	'The Masked Philosopher', in Lawrence D. Kritzman (ed.), Michel Foucault (1988), *Politics, Philosophy, Culture: Interviews and Other Writings 1977–1984*, New York and London: Routledge, pp. 323–30.
NGH:	'Nietzsche, Genealogy, History', in Michel Foucault (1977), *Language, Counter-Memory, Practice: Selected Essays and Interviews*, Donald F. Bouchard (ed.), New York: Cornell University Press, pp. 139–64.
OP:	'On Power', in Lawrence D. Kritzman (ed.), Michel Foucault (1988), *Politics, Philosophy, Culture: Interviews and Other Writings 1977–1984*, New York and London: Routledge, pp. 96–109.
PC:	'Practicing Criticism', in Lawrence D. Kritzman (ed.), Michel Foucault (1988), *Politics, Philosophy, Culture: Interviews and Other Writings 1977–1984*, New York and London: Routledge, pp. 152–6.
PE:	'Politics and Ethics: An Interview', in Paul Rabinow (ed.) (1984), *The Foucault Reader*, London: Penguin, pp. 373–80.

PHS: 'Preface to The History of Sexuality, Volume 2', in Michel Foucault (1997), *Ethics: Subjectivity and Truth, The Essential Works of Michel Foucault 1954–1984*, Vol. 1, Paul Rabinow (ed.), London: Penguin, pp. 199–205.

PPP: 'Polemics, Politics, and Problematizations: An Interview', in Michel Foucault (1997), *Ethics: Subjectivity and Truth, The Essential Works of Michel Foucault 1954–1984*, Vol. 1, Paul Rabinow (ed.), London: Penguin, pp. 111–19.

PS: 'Power and Sex', in Lawrence D. Kritzman (ed.), Michel Foucault (1988), *Politics, Philosophy, Culture: Interviews and Other Writings 1977–1984*, New York and London: Routledge, pp. 110–24.

PST: 'Power and Strategies', in Michel Foucault (1980), *Power/Knowledge: Selected Interviews and Other Writings 1972–1977*, Colin Gordon (ed.), New York: Pantheon Books, pp. 134–45.

PT: 'Prison Talk', in Michel Foucault (1980), *Power/Knowledge: Selected Interviews and Other Writings 1972–1977*, Colin Gordon (ed.), New York: Pantheon Books, pp. 37–54.

QM: 'Questions of Method', in Graham Burchell et al. (1991), *The Foucault Effect: Studies in Governmentality*, Chicago: Chicago University Press, pp. 73–86.

SCA: 'Sexual Choice, Sexual Act: Foucault and Homosexuality', in Lawrence D. Kritzman (ed.), Michel Foucault (1988), *Politics, Philosophy, Culture: Interviews and Other Writings 1977–1984*, New York and London: Routledge, pp. 286–303.

SKP: 'Space, Knowledge, and Power', in Paul Rabinow (ed.) (1984), *The Foucault Reader*, London: Penguin, pp. 239–56.

SP: 'The Subject and Power', Afterword in Hubert L. Dreyfus and Paul Rabinow (eds) (1982), *Michel Foucault: Beyond Structuralism and hermeneutics*, Brighton: The Harvester Press, pp. 208–26.

SPI: 'Sex, Power, and the Politics of Identity', in Michel Foucault (1997), *Ethics: Subjectivity and Truth, The Essential Works of Michel Foucault 1954–1984*, Vol. 1, Paul Rabinow (ed.), London: Penguin, pp. 163–73.

SPS: 'Structuralism and Post-structuralism', in Michel Foucault (1998), *Aesthetics, Method, and Epistemology, The Essential Works of Michel Foucault 1954–1984*, Vol. 2, James D. Faubion (ed.), London: Penguin, pp. 433–58.

ST: 'Subjectivity and Truth', in Michel Foucault (2007), *The Politics of Truth*, Sylvère Lotringer (ed.), Los Angeles: Semiotext(e), pp. 147–67.

THS: 'The History of Sexuality', in Michel Foucault (1980), *Power/Knowledge: Selected Interviews and Other Writings 1972–1977*, Colin Gordon (ed.), New York: Pantheon Books, pp. 183–93.

TJF: 'Truth and Juridical Forms', in Michel Foucault (2000), *Power, The Essential Works of Michel Foucault 1954–1984*, Vol. 3, James D. Faubion (ed.), New York: The New Press, pp. 1–89.

TL: 'Two Lectures', in Michel Foucault (1980), *Power/Knowledge: Selected Interviews and Other Writings 1972–1977*, Colin Gordon (ed.), New York: Pantheon Books, pp. 78–108.

TP: 'Truth and Power', in Michel Foucault (1980), *Power/Knowledge: Selected Interviews and Other Writings 1972–1977*, Colin Gordon (ed.), New York: Pantheon Books, pp. 109–33.

UR: 'Useless to Revolt?' in Michel Foucault (2000), *Power, The Essential Works of Michel Foucault 1954–1984*, Vol. 3, James D. Faubion (ed.), New York: The New Press, pp. 449–53.

WC: 'What Is Critique?' in Michel Foucault (2007), *The Politics of Truth*, Sylvère Lotringer (ed.), Los Angeles: Semiotext(e), pp. 41–81.

WE: 'What Is Enlightenment?', in Michel Foucault (2007), *The Politics of Truth*, Sylvère Lotringer (ed.), Los Angeles: Semiotext(e), pp. 97–119.

References

Others

Allen, Barry (1998). 'Foucault and Modern Political Philosophy', in Jeremy Moss (ed.), *The Later Foucault*, London: Sage, pp. 164–98.

Arendt, Hannah (1968). *Between Past and Future*, London: Penguin.

Bernstein, Richard J. (1991). *The New Constellation*, Cambridge: Polity Press.

Blencowe, Claire (2012). *Biopolitical Experience: Foucault, Power and Positive Critique*, Houndmills: Palgrave Macmillan.

Brökling, Ulrich, Susanne Krasmann and Thomas Lemke (2011). 'From Foucault's Lectures at the Collège de France to Studies of Governmentality: An Introduction', in Ulrich Brökling, Susanne

Krasmann and Thomas Lemke (eds), *Governmentality: Current Issues and Future Challenges*, London: Routledge, pp. 1–33.

Brown, Peter (1992). *Power and Persuasion in Late Antiquity: Towards a Christian Empire*, Madison, Wisconsin: The University of Wisconsin Press.

Clifford, Michael (2001). *Political Genealogy after Foucault: Savage Identities*, New York and London: Routledge.

Dahl, Robert A. (1968). 'A Critique of the Ruling Elite Model', in G. William Domhoff and Hoyt B. Ballard (eds), *C. Wright Mills and The Power Elite*, Boston: Beacon Press, pp. 25–36.

Dean, Mitchell (1994). *Critical and Effective Histories: Foucault's Methods and Historical Sociology*, New York and London : Routledge.

Deleuze, Gilles (1986). *Foucault*, Paris: Les Édition de Minuit

Dews, Peter (1986). 'The *Nouvelle Philosophie* and Foucault', in Mike Gane (ed.), *Towards a Critique of Foucault*, New York and London : Routledge, pp. 81–105.

Derrida, Jacques (1976). *Of Grammatology*, Baltimore and London: The Johns Hopkins University Press.

Doxiadis, Kyrkos (1997). 'Foucault and the Three-headed King: State, Ideology and Theory as Targets of Critique', *Economy and Society*, Vol. 26, No. 4, pp. 518–45.

Dyrberg, Torben Bech (1997). *The Circular Structure of Power: Politics, Identity, Community*, London: Verso.

Dyrberg, Torben Bech (2009). 'The Leftist Fascination with Schmitt and the Esoteric Quality of "the Political" ', *Philosophy and Social Criticism*, Vol. 35, No. 6, pp. 649–69.

Easton, David (1953). *The Political System: An Inquiry into the State of Political Science*, New York: Alfred A Knopf.

Eribon, Didier (1991). *Michel Foucault*, Harvard: Harvard University Press.

Etzioni-Halevy, Eva (1993). *The Elite Connection*, Cambridge: Polity Press.

Etzioni-Halevy, Eva (1997). 'Elites and the Working Class', in Eva Etzioni-Halevy (ed.), *Classes and Elites in Democracy and Democratization*, London: Routledge, pp. 310–26.

Falzon, Christopher (1998). *Foucault and Social Dialogue: Beyond Fragmentation*, London: Routledge.

Farrell, Clare (1989). *Foucault? Historian or Philosopher?* Houndmills: Palgrave Macmillan.

Faubion, James D. (2011). *An Anthropology of Ethics*, Cambridge: Cambridge University Press.
Fine, Bob (1979). 'Struggles against Discipline: The Theory and Politics of Michel Foucault, *Capital and Class*, No. 9, pp. 75–96.
Fine, Bob (1984). *Democracy and the Rule of Law*, London: Pluto Press.
Fleischacker, Samuel (2013). *What Is Enlightenment?* London: Routledge.
Flynn, Thomas R. (2005). *Sartre, Foucault, and Historical Reason*, Vol. 2: *A Poststructuralist Mapping of History*, Chicago: The University of Chicago Press.
Fraser, Nancy (1981). 'Foucault on Modern Power: Empirical Insights and Normative Confusions', *Praxis International*, Vol. 1, No. 3, pp. 272–87.
Giddens, Anthony (1979). *Central Problems in Social Theory*, London: Palgrave Macmillan.
Goldstein, R. J. (1991). 'Preface: Changing One's Mind', in Michel Foucault, *Remarks on Marx*, Conversations with Duccio Trombarodi, New York: Semiotext(e), pp. 7–14.
Gordon, Colin (1987). 'The Soul of the Citizen: Max Weber and Michel Foucault on Rationality and Government', in Sam Whimster and Scott Lash (eds), *Max Weber, Rationality and Modernity*, London: Allen and Unwin, pp. 293–316.
Gros, Frédéric (2005). 'Course Context', in Michel Foucault, *The Hermeneutics of the Subject*, Lectures at the Collège de France 1981–1982, New York: Picador, pp. 507–50.
Habermas, Jürgen (1971). 'Der Universalitätsanspruch der Hermeneutik', in Karl-Otto Apel et al. (eds), *Hermeneutik und Ideologiekritik*, Frankfurt: Suhrkamp Verlag, pp. 120–59.
Hardt, Michael (2010). 'Militant Life', *New Left Review*, No. 64, pp. 151–60.
Hendricks, Christina (2012). 'Prophecy and Parresia: Foucauldian Critique and the Political Role of Intellectuals', in Karin de Boer and Ruth Sonderegger (eds), *Conceptions of Critique in Modern and Contemporary Philosophy*, Houndmills: Palgrave Macmillan, pp. 212–30.
Hook, Derek (2007). *Foucault, Psychology and the Analytics of Power*, Houndmills: Palgrave Macmillan.
Hoy, David Couzens (1979). 'Taking History Seriously: Foucault, Gadamer, Habermas', *Union Seminary Quarterly Review*, Vol. 34, No. 2, pp. 85–95.

Hoy, David Couzens (1998). 'Foucault and Critical Theory', in Jeremy Moss (ed.), *The Later Foucault*, London: Sage, pp. 18–32.
Hoy, David Couzens (2004). *Critical Resistance: From Poststructuralism to Post-Critique*, Cambridge, Mass. and London: The MIT Press.
Jameson, Fredric (1998). *The Cultural Turn*, London: Verso.
Jenkins, Laura (2011). 'The Difference Genealogy Makes: Strategies for Politicisation or How to Extend Capacities for Autonomy', *Political Studies*, Vol. 59, No. 1, pp. 156–74.
Jessop, Bob (1987). 'Poulantzas and Foucault on Power and Strategy', *Ideas and Production*, No. 6, pp. 59–84.
Jessop, Bob (2011). 'Constituting Another Foucault Effect: Foucault on States and Statecraft', in Ulrich Brökling, Susanne Krasmann and Thomas Lemke (eds), *Governmentality: Current Issues and Future Challenges*, London: Routledge, pp. 56–73.
Kant, Immanuel (1997). 'Was ist Aufklärung?', in Michel Foucault (1997), *The Politics of Truth*, edited by Sylvère Lotringer, Los Angeles: Semiotext(e), pp. 29–37.
Keat, Russell (1986). 'Foucault and the Repressive Hypothesis', *Radical Philosophy*, 42, pp. 24–32.
Kelly, Mark G. E. (2013). *Foucault's History of Sexuality Volume I, The Will to Knowledge*. Edinburgh: Edinburgh University Press.
Kromann, Joakim and Thomas Klem Andersen (2011). 'Parresia: The Problem of Truth, *Ephemera*, Vol. 11, No. 2, pp. 225–30.
Laclau, Ernesto (1990). *New Reflections on the Revolution of Our Time*, London: Verso.
Laclau, Ernesto and Chantal Mouffe (1985). *Hegemony and Socialist Strategy*, London: Verso.
Lakoff, George (2008). *The Political Mind*, New York: Viking.
Lazzarato, Maurizio (2013). 'Enunciation and Politics: A Parallel Reading of Democracy', in Jakob Nilsson and Sven-Olov Wallenstein (eds), *Foucault, Biopolitics and Governmentality*, Huddinge: Södertörn Philosophical Studies, pp. 155–73.
Lemke, Thomas (2012). *Foucault, Governmentality, and Critique*, Boulder: Paradigm Publishers.
Lukes, Steven (2005). *Power a Radical View*, Second Edition, Houndmills: Palgrave Macmillan.
Lynch, Richard A. (2011). 'Foucault's Theory of Power', in Dianna Taylor (ed.), *Michel Foucault: Key Concepts*, Durham: Acumen, pp. 13–26.

Markovits, Elizabeth (2008). *The Politics of Sincerity: Plato, Frank Speech, and Democratic Judgment*, Pennsylvania: The Pennsylvania State University Press.

May, Todd (1993). *Between Genealogy and Epistemology: Psychology, Politics, and Knowledge in the Thought of Michel Foucault*, Pennsylvania: The Pennsylvania State University Press.

McNay, Lois (1994). *Foucault: A Critical Introduction*, Cambridge: Polity Press.

Mendieta, Eduardo (2011). 'The Practice of Freedom', in Dianna Taylor (ed.), *Michel Foucault: Key Concepts*, Durham: Acumen, pp. 111–24.

Miller, James (1994). *The Passion of Michel Foucault*, London: Flamingo.

Miller, Paul Allen (2006). 'Truth-Telling in Foucault's "Le gouvernement de soi et des autres" and Persius 1: The Subject, Rhetoric, and Power', *Parrhesia*, No. 1, pp. 27–61.

Morriss, Peter (1987). *Power: A Philosophical Analysis*, Manchester: Manchester University Press.

Morriss, Peter (2006). 'Steven Lukes on the Concept of Power', *Political Studies Review*, Vol. 4, No. 2, pp. 124–35.

Neocleous, Mark (1996). *Administering Civil Society*, Houndmills: Palgrave Macmillan.

Nikolinakos, Derek D. (1990). 'Foucault's Ethical Quandary', *Telos*, No. 83, pp. 123–40.

Norris, Christopher (1994). '"What Is Enlightenment?" Kant and Foucault', in Gary Gutting (ed.), *The Cambridge Companion to Foucault*, Cambridge: Cambridge University Press, pp. 159–96.

Oksala, Johanna (2005). *Foucault on Freedom*, Cambridge: Cambridge University Press.

Oksala, Johanna (2007). *How to Read Foucault*, London: Granta Books.

O'Leary, Timothy (2010). 'Rethinking Experience with Foucault', in Timothy O'Leary and Christopher Falzon (eds), *Foucault and Philosophy*, Chichester: Wiley-Blackwell, pp. 162–84.

O'Neill, John (1987). 'The Disciplinary Society: From Weber to Foucault', *The British Journal of Sociology*, Vol. 37, No. 1, pp. 42–60.

Owen, David (1999). 'Orientation and Enlightenment: An Essay on Critique and Genealogy', in Samantha Ashenden and David Owen (eds), *Foucault Contra Habermas*, London: Sage, pp. 21–44.

Owen, David (2002). 'Criticism and Captivity: On Genealogy and Critical Theory', *European Journal of Philosophy*, Vol. 10, No. 2, pp. 216–30.

Paras, Eric (2006). *Foucault 2.0: Beyond Power and Knowledge*, New York: Other Press.

Patton, Paul (1989). 'Taylor and Foucault on Power and Freedom', *Political Studies*, Vol. 37, pp. 260–76.

Patton, Paul (2003). 'Foucault', in David Boucher and Paul Kelly (eds), *Political Thinkers: From Socrates to the Present*, Oxford: Oxford University Press, pp. 516–35.

Patton, Paul (2005). 'Foucault, Critique and Rights', *Critical Horizons*, Vol. 6, No. 1, pp. 267–87.

Patton, Paul (2010). 'Foucault and Normative Political Philosophy: Liberal and Neo-Liberal Governmentality and Public Reason', in Timothy O'Leary and Christopher Falzon (eds), *Foucault and Philosophy*, Chichester: Wiley-Blackwell, pp. 204–21.

Philp Mark (1983). 'Foucault on Power: A Problem in Radical Translation', *Political Theory*, Vol. 11, No. 1, pp. 29–52.

Poulantzas, Nicos (1978). *State, Power, Socialism*, London: Verso.

Racevskis, Karlis (1983). *Michel Foucault and the Subversion of Intellect*, Ithaca and London: Cornell University Press.

Rajchman, John (1985). *The Freedom of Philosophy*, New York: Columbia University Press.

Ransom, John S. (1997). *Foucault's Discipline: The Politics of Subjectivity*, Durham and London: Duke University Press.

Rawls, John (1993). *Political Liberalism*, New York: Columbia University Press.

Rawls, John (1995). 'Reply to Habermas', *The Journal of Philosophy*, Vol. 42, No. 3, pp. 132–80.

Rayner, Timothy (2010). 'Foucault, Heidegger, and the History of Truth', in Timothy O'Leary and Christopher Falzon (eds), *Foucault and Philosophy*, Chichester: Wiley-Blackwell, pp. 60–77.

Redhead, Mark (2010). 'Complimenting Rivals: Foucault, Rawls and the Problem of Public Reasoning', *Western Political Science Association 2010 Annual Meeting Paper*, 23 pages.

Saar, Martin (2002). 'Genealogy and Subjectivity', *European Journal of Philosophy*, Vol. 10, No. 2, pp. 231–45.

Saxonhouse, Arlene W. (2006). *Free Speech and Democracy in Ancient Athens*, Cambridge: Cambridge University Press.

Schirato, Tony, Geoff Danaher and Jen Webb (2012). *Understanding Foucault*, London: Sage.

Simons, Jon (1995). *Foucault and the Political*, New York and London : Routledge.

Sluga, Hans (2011). 'Could You Define the Sense You Give the Word "Political"'? Michel Foucault as a Political Philosopher', *History of the Human Sciences*, Vol. 24, No. 1, pp. 69–79.

Smart, Barry (1983). *Foucault, Marxism and Critique*, London: Routledge.

Szakolczai, Arpad (2003). *The Genesis of Modernity*, London: Routledge.

Stone, Brad Elliott (2011). 'Subjectivity and Truth', in Dianna Taylor (ed.), *Michel Foucault: Key Concepts*, Durham: Acumen, pp. 143–57.

Veyne, Paul (2010). *Foucault: His Thought, His Character*, Cambridge: Polity Press.

Villadsen, Kaspar and Mitchell Dean (2012). 'State-Phobia, Civil Society, and a Certain Vitalism', *Constellations*, Vol. 19, No. 3, pp. 401–20.

Vogelmann, Frieder (2012). 'Foucaults parrhesia – Philosophie als Politik der Wahrheit', in Petra Gehring and Andreas Gelhard (eds), *Parrhesia: Foucault und der Mut zur Wahrheit*, Zürich: Diaphanes, pp. 203–29.

Weber, Max (1978). *Economy and Society*, Vol. 2, Guenther Roth and Claus Wittich (eds), Berkeley: University of California Press.

Wickham, Gary (1986). 'Power and Power Analysis: Beyond Foucault', in Mike Gane (ed.), *Towards a Critique of Foucault*, New York and London : Routledge, pp. 149–79.

Williams, Bernard (1996). 'Truth, Politics, and Self-Deception', *Social Research*, Vol. 63, No. 3, pp. 603–17.

Williams, Bernard (2002). *Truth and Truthfulness: An Essay in Genealogy*, Princeton: Princeton University Press.

Wolin, Richard (2010). *The Wind From the East: French Intellectuals, the Cultural Revolution, and the Legacy of the 1960s*, Princeton and Oxford: Princeton University Press.

Index

acceptable/unacceptable, 33
acceptance, 2, 50, 67, 72-3, 79, 117
accountability, 2, 67, 90
agonism, 26, 118
agonistic, 24, 28, 35, 37, 46-7, 61, 68, 84-5, 91-2, 106, 111-5, 117-8
Althusser, Louis, 38
analytical philosophy, 44n6
antiquity, 16, 73, 85, 93
archaeological method, 56-7
Arendt, Hannah, 8, 64n9, 82, 106
ascendance, 74, 85, 91
authenticity, 51
authority, 22, 43, 52, 67, 98-9, 117
authority/laypeople axis, 3, 5, 8, 13, 17, 32, 37, 52, 70, 73, 80, 111, 124
autonomy, 49, 54, 69, 71, 80, 85, 89, 92, 95, 97, 105, 106, 120

becoming, 34-5, 36
Bernstein, Richard, 81-2
bio-politics, 12, 25, 26, 123

capitalism, 17, 38, 40
censorship, 85, 91, 107
Chomsky, Noam, 25, 38
Christianity, 99-100
civil society, 5, 79, 86, 101n2
class consciousness, 50
class domination, 19, 38-9, 40

codes of conduct, 13
coercion, 39, 42, 114
command/obedience relations, 5-6
communal life, 97-100
communism, 60
community, 36, 70, 88, 102-18
comprehensive doctrines, 43, 50, 60, 77, 94-5, 106, 108, 116
conflict, 5, 8, 19, 43, 49
conflicts of interest, 13, 14
conformity, 6, 54, 62, 85, 91, 100, 107, 118, 120
consensus, 43, 49
control, 4, 18, 21-4, 26-8, 39, 52-3, 60, 98, 108, 123-4
counterculture, 69
courage/courageous, 2, 34-6, 49, 51, 54, 64n8, 65n11, 66-9, 71-2, 78, 81, 85, 87, 90-1, 96, 98-100, 108, 111-3, 125
critical engagement, 2, 4, 8, 10, 13, 31-2, 34, 54-9
critical ontology, 53, 55, 59-63
critical theory, 5, 24, 32, 33, 42, 50, 69, 77, 83n8
critique, 2, 6-8, 13, 27, 67
  genealogical, 34, 37
  ideology, 24, 32, 33, 37-43, 47, 48, 49-50, 93-4
  nature of, 31-45, 78
  political, 32-5, 50-4
  politics of, 46-65
curiosity, 35, 36, 57-8, 81

Dahl, Robert A., 15–16, 21
Deleuze, Gilles, 29n3
deliberative democracy, 32
democracy, 2–3, 6, 7, 13, 52, 55, 69
 deliberative, 32
 ethical differentiation and, 104–7
 parrhesia and, 71, 72, 78, 79–82, 85–91, 103–4
 pluralist, 36
democratic paradoxes, 107–13
democratic ethos, 3, 7, 74, 103, 110
democratic political community, 3, 54, 115
democratic politics, 79–82
democratic theory, 13
demo–elitism, 113–18
demonstrative truth, 94, 95, 96, 116, 120
depoliticization, 124–5
Derrida, Jacques, 22
desubjectivation, 34, 55, 56, 65n11
disciplinary subjection, 5–6, 18
disciplinary technologies, 14, 18, 122
discipline, 18, 25, 38, 39, 64n10, 74
Discipline and Punish (Foucault), 15, 17, 29n3
discursive practices, 72, 73, 75, 76, 82n6
domination, 2, 4, 5, 8, 11, 14, 17–29, 33, 47, 48, 51–2, 70, 99, 116, 120
dunasteia, 111

effective history, 6
elites/elite theory, 15–16, 21, 23, 103, 113–18
emancipatory politics, 52, 96
enlightenment, 49, 55, 64n8, 67, 85
enlightenment ethos, 2, 37, 56, 59, 67, 81, 85
equality, 3, 6–7, 23, 39, 71, 74–5, 78, 80, 89, 99, 101n3, 102–3, 105, 108–10, 116–7
essentialism, 47, 55
ethical differentiation, 104–7
ethical practices, 35–7

ethics, 2, 11, 26–7, 30n7, 47, 54, 67, 72–7, 79, 95
ethos, 34
Etzioni-Halevy, Eva, 114, 115
experience, 76
experimentation, 35, 36
exploitation, 52

false consciousness, 41, 42
false knowledge, 40–1
fear, 6, 33, 85, 91, 100
flattery, 103, 104, 105, 111, 113
force relations, 121–3
Foucault, Michel
 on critique, 31–45, 50–4
 on ideology, 39–43
 on *parrhesia*, 3–6, 8–9, 66–83
 as political theorist, 6–8, 9
 on politics, 5
 on power, 3–4, 5, 10–31
 frame of reference, 36
Frankfurt School, 83n8
freedom, 26, 28, 54–8, 60, 61, 68, 98, 99
 see also liberty
 degrees of, 25, 27–8
free speech, 71, 79, 90, 100, 115

genealogical critique, 34, 37
Giddens, Anthony, 29n1
governance, 48–54, 67
government, 15, 25, 74, 87
governmentality, 47, 49, 61, 62, 103–4, 105, 123
grand theory, 56
Gros, Frederic, 24

Habermas, Jürgen, 32, 43, 77, 87, 113
habits, 56
hegemony, 43
Heidegger, Martin, 43n1
hierarchy, 48, 96, 97–100, 107, 116, 120, 123
history, 47
hypocrisy, 100

Index 139

ideal speech situation, 113
identity, 36
identity politics, 5, 7, 36, 48
ideology critique, 32, 33, 37–43, 47–50, 93–4
illegitimacy, 62
individuality, 24, 106–7
institutional capacities, 12
institutions, 57, 107, 121, 123
integrity, 99
interest groups, 5, 7, 14
isegoria, 109–10, 112, 120
isonomia, 120

Kant, Immanuel, 47, 49, 51, 55, 83n8
knowledge, 2, 11, 15, 42, 47, 57, 110, 122
  illusion of, 95–6
  power, ethics, and, 72–7
  true vs. false, 40–1

Laclau, Ernesto, 30n8, 44n2
law, 59, 61
laypeople, 3, 5, 8, 17, 32, 34, 37, 52, 70, 73, 80, 111, 115
leadership/community relationship, 102–18
legitimacy, 62, 72
liberalism, 59, 85, 104
liberty, 2–3, 5–6, 19, 23, 26–8, 33, 39, 51, 56, 61, 70–1, 74, 85, 95–6, 101n3, 105, 108, 110, 114, 116–7
liberty and equality, 39, 74, 101n3, 105, 108, 110, 114, 116–7
  see also freedom
limits, 12–13, 34–5, 55, 58

Markovits, Elizabeth, 86
Marxism, 15, 17, 37, 39–40, 48, 56, 59, 96, 103
meritocracy, 71
Miller, Paul Allen, 89
moral codes, 35–7
morals, 30n7

Nietzsche, Friedrich, 6, 9, 19, 26, 32, 36, 47, 93
normalization, 39, 51, 52, 73
normative theories, 34, 35, 37, 42, 77
norms, 34, 86
Norris, Christopher, 54

obedience, 2, 3, 6, 38, 97–100, 118, 120
objectivation, 58, 116
objectivity, 47
ontology of the present, 44n6
openness, 56, 68
Owen, David, 43

parrhesia, 27
  concept of, 2–6
  democracy and, 71, 72, 78, 79–82, 85–91, 103–4
  democratic paradoxes and, 107–13
  as demo-elitism, 113–18
  Foucault on, 3–6, 8–9, 66–83
  Foucault's interest in, 77–9
  framing of, 112
  methodological considerations in studying, 72–7
  nature of, 66–83
  political aspect of, 2–3
  political ethos of, 68–9
  political exclusion and, 91–7
  politics of, 84–101, 120–5
parrhesiastic pact, 86–91, 99
perspectivism, 68
persuasion, 88
Plato, 93, 103, 109
pluralism, 68, 113–14
pluralist democracy, 36
polemics, 117–18
political analytics, 69–72
political authorities, 32–4, 37, 70, 80, 111, 115, 121
political authority, 3–4, 7–8, 32, 61, 85, 97
political community, 4, 7, 68, 80, 92, 98–9, 114–5, 118, 124
political critique, 32–5, 50–4
political economy, 62

DOI: 10.1057/9781137368355.0012

political ethics, 54, 67, 79
political ethos, 68–72
political exclusion, 91–7
political orientation, 59–63
political power, 3–5, 7, 14, 16, 19, 23–4, 70, 74, 78, 87, 108, 124
political practice, 69–72, 79, 96
political reasoning, 106–7, 116
political relations, 4–6
political subjectivation, 2
political theory, 6–8, 9, 32
politicization, 124–5
politics
  autonomy of, 85, 89, 94, 96, 106, 120
  bio-politics, 12, 25, 26, 123
  of critical engagement, 54–9
  of critique, 46–65
  democratic, 79–82
  domain of, 120–5
  emancipatory, 52, 96
  as freestanding, 91–7
  identity, 36, 48
  interest group, 5, 7, 14
  of *parrhesia*, 84–101
  of truth, 33, 42
  of truth-telling, 2, 5–6, 66–83, 98, 105
positivism, 58
post-politics context, 47–8
Poulantzas, Nicos, 38
power, 2–5
  abuses of, 28
  as discipline, 18
  domination and, 11, 14, 17–29, 33, 47, 74
  Foucault on, 10–31
  knowledge, ethics, and, 72–7
  marginalization of, 113
  political, 7, 14, 16, 19, 23–4, 70, 74, 78, 87, 108, 124
  politics of, 15–17
  as productive submission, 12, 14–18, 24
  resistance to, 33, 34, 49, 69
  speaking truth to, 71

sub-categories of, 12
supplementary, 44n5
theories of, 11, 15–17
transformative capacity of, 12–13
use/abuse of, 28, 91–2
Weber on, 21–2
power analytics, 11, 13–14, 15
power over, 26, 97
power relations, 7–8, 12, 14–16, 20–8, 37, 38, 43, 70, 74–5, 120–4
power to, 26
pragmatism, 61
primacy, 72
prisons, 37, 72, 73
problematization, 70
productive submission, 8, 10, 12, 14–18, 20, 24, 26, 33, 37, 39, 69, 122
progress, 19, 37, 47, 57
prophecy, 93
psychiatry, 58–9
public political reasoning, 2, 7, 28, 52, 86, 94–5, 103, 105–7, 116–7

radical, 3, 5–6, 9, 15–7, 25, 28, 31–2, 36, 46–51, 54–5, 59–60, 62–3, 65n12, 65n13, 97, 103, 124
radicalism, 15–16, 59, 62–3
Rawls, John, 7, 8, 32, 43, 59, 87, 108, 117
reactivation, 30n8
reason, 85
reductionism, 76
reflected intractability, 33
reflexivity, 35, 75, 79
regime structures, 4, 70, 115–16
relationalism, 76
religion, 94, 99–100
religious dogmatism, 72, 120
repression, 18, 19, 23–5
resistance, 8, 11, 15, 18–23, 28, 33, 34, 37, 47, 49, 69
revolution, 59, 61, 62, 63, 65n12
rhetoric, 103, 104, 113
rules, 13, 56

Schmitt, Carl, 48
science, 40–1

secularization thesis, 92–3, 94
security, 12, 25
sedimentation, 30n8
self-care, 12, 92, 94
self-determination, 54
self-esteem, 79
self-interest, 4, 80, 103
sexuality, 73, 76–7
Sluga, Hans, 120
social contract, 61
socialism, 51
social relations, 12
social status, 94
social stratification, 95, 116, 120
society, political infrastructure of, 3–4
sovereignty, 25, 39, 51–2, 60, 61
special interests, 32
subaltern groups, 48
subject, 11, 26–7, 75, 90
subjectivity, 35–6, 96
sublimation of cruelty, 37–8
submission, 19, 96, 122
supplementary power, 44n5
surveillance, 39, 51, 52
system, 37

tolerable/intolerable, 33
toleration, 79

tradition, 36
transgression, 12–13, 34–5, 41, 55, 58, 62
true/false distinction, 73
trustworthiness, 2, 67, 85, 89, 98, 120
truth, 33, 40–1, 42, 67, 86–7, 91
  analytics of, 49
  demonstrative, 94, 95, 96, 116, 120
  forms of, 95–6
  games, 52, 59
  history of, 49
  production of, 73, 74–5, 76
truthfulness, 85, 120
truth-telling, 4, 11, 12, 95
  politics of, 2, 5–6, 66–83, 98, 105
  reasons for, 78–9
tyranny, 104

universalism, 47
utilitarianism, 62

veto power, 72
violence, 123
voluntary insubordination, 33

Wahr-sagen, 75
war, 19, 23
Weber, Max, 21–2, 27
working class, 40